The Ultimate Joy

A Journey in Intimacy with God

Judy Mills

WestBow
PRESS
A DIVISION OF THOMAS NELSON

WestBow Press books may be ordered through booksellers or by contacting:

WestBow Press
A Division of Thomas Nelson
1663 Liberty Drive
Bloomington, IN 47403
www.westbowpress.com
1-(866) 928-1240

Because of the dynamic nature of the Internet, any web addresses or links contained in this book may have changed since publication and may no longer be valid. The views expressed in this work are solely those of the author and do not necessarily reflect the views of the publisher, and the publisher hereby disclaims any responsibility for them.

Any people depicted in stock imagery provided by Thinkstock are models, and such images are being used for illustrative purposes only.

Certain stock imagery © Thinkstock.

ISBN: 978-1-4497-6517-0 (sc)

Library of Congress Control Number: 2012915938

Printed in the United States of America

WestBow Press rev. date: 1/21/2013

Contents

Introduction

"God, You must not want that with me."

As best I can recall, those were the exact words I spoke to God in December 1993. I had just completed Henry Blackaby's Bible study *Experiencing God*, which is a wonderful course during which my fellow students shared how they had experienced intimacy with God. I marveled at their experiences yet was saddened that I didn't share such intimacy with Him. My conclusion was, "God, You must not want that with me."

Even now, many years later, I vividly recall those words and the decision I made to cool it with God. I hadn't stopped believing in Him, and neither did I doubt my personal salvation. I had simply determined that there was a level of intimacy with God that was enjoyed by some, but they were a group for which I had apparently not been chosen. The tender emotions I felt then still linger—emotions not only of pain but also joy as God began revealing that He did want a relationship of intimacy with me.

God wants intimacy with you too. He's been pursuing intimacy with mankind since the beginning. He set up the times and places you would live so you would seek it with Him. Psalm 16:11 is a key passage for this study: "You have made known to me the path of life; You fill me with joy in Your presence, with eternal pleasures at Your right hand."

There is so much God wants to make known to you—so much of Himself He wants to share with you. There is great joy and God-filled pleasure He wants to give you.

As I reflect back over the year 1994, I remember how I craved time with God. I recall no thoughts of things I would do for Him or things He would do for me. I only wanted to be with Him, for I was beginning to understand how much He loved and wanted to be with me.

God has set each one of us on a path of life—a path that can be our journey into ever-deepening intimacy with Him. My prayer is that this study will propel you in your journey into intimacy with God.

Week 1
The Pursuit

Intimacy—an affectionate, loving personal relationship with another person. The feeling of belonging together; having a detailed knowledge and deep understanding of one another. The absence of walls or fences.[1]

Day 1
Evaluating Our Pursuit

It was a January morning when the words fell clearly on my heart: the ultimate joy in life is found in intimacy with God. The words came after months (really years) of letting go. Letting go of a ministry role I dearly loved and thoroughly enjoyed. Letting go of things I wanted to be and to do. Letting go of what I wanted people to think of me. In letting go, I had made room for what I truly, though unknowingly, desired. It's what you and I were made for: a relationship of intimacy with God.

We fill our lives with many things: people, places, work, church, ministry, sports, exercise, books, movies, television, endeavors, projects, meetings, appointments, engagements, commitments. We form groups and join clubs. We affiliate, congregate, and collect friends on social networks. We make money, spend money, fret over the lack of money, and spend time deciding how to invest and to whom we should leave our money.

We are busy! We keep busy, feel too busy, and don't understand how life has become so busy. We perform, strive, go for it, and just do it. We compare and compete; we fail and succeed. We make plans, change plans, stick very closely to our plans, and dare anyone or anything to interfere with our plans.

A full calendar means a full life—right? Success means we are doing well in this life. Happiness is proof that we've done enough good things so we can enjoy life, right? Yet deep inside we are still full of longings. We long:

> To belong and to have purpose.
> To know and be known.
> To understand and be understood.
> To accept and be accepted.
> To care and be cared for.
> To love and be loved.

What we long for is intimacy. We long for intimacy because we were made for intimacy. Yet we often pursue other things and miss the fact that our longings are finally and fully satisfied only in a relationship of intimacy with God. God designed us for it. He calls us to it. Jesus came and showed it to us and then made a way for us to have it.

God's invitation to intimacy is a summons for you to know Him. Read the definition of intimacy on page one again. It's a request to be in an affectionate, loving, unique, intimate relationship with Him. It's a relationship that even exceeds a sense of belonging together! It grows into oneness as barriers come down through time spent together.

The question is:

> Will you pursue it?

Do you desire it? Will you make room in your schedule and in your heart for it? In the days ahead, you will see God's incredible pursuit of you, but for today, consider the nature of your pursuit of Him. A very precious promise is given in James 4:8: "Draw near to God and He will draw near to you." This New Testament verse is similar to an Old Testament promise given to the nation of Israel during a time when it had turned away from God. The heart of the promise is for us also, even if we have turned away from God: "You will seek Me and find Me when you seek Me with all your heart. I will be found by you" (Jer. 29:13–14a).

The best starting point for this study is for you to spend time sharing with God your thoughts on the intimacy or lack of intimacy you currently have with Him. Be honest with Him, for in doing so you are also being honest with yourself.

Use the following space and to the side to write a prayer to God.

Day 2
Making It the Main Event

At the Peachtree Road Race held every Fourth of July in Atlanta, Georgia, event planners strategically place water stations every mile along the 6.2-mile route. These stations are designed to assist runners in staying hydrated during the race. They often have not only water but a sports drink and even sports gels (that are gummy-like and full of carbohydrates) ready and waiting through the assistance of eager volunteers. These volunteers also spur you on through their cheers and encouraging words. The road race is the event; it's why the participants are there. They don't come for the water, the gels, or to hang out with the volunteers at the water station, though they are thankful for the assistance and encouragement. Imagine for a minute how odd the scene would be if runners chose to stop at a water station and spend the rest of the race there.

Spiritually speaking, is that what we have done? The things we fill our lives with could be compared to these water stations—even the Bible studies and church activities with which so many of us fill our time. They exist to assist, equip, encourage, and spur us on, but they are not the main event. God is to be our number-one pursuit. He is the main event!

In John 17:3, Jesus says, "This is eternal life: that they know You, the one true God, and Jesus Christ whom You sent." Our specific journey is the way in which He has chosen for us to know and come into oneness with Him. The apostle Paul understood this. In Philippians 3, he shares part of his journey.

Read Philippians 3, and answer the following questions.

Describe Paul's life when he put confidence in the flesh and sought to fill himself with earthly things (3:4–6):

Paul sought many things, some bad and some good, but in 3:8, he makes a very bold statement. Using verses 3:7–11, summarize Paul's words:

Since God's invitation to intimacy is an invitation to know Him, let's take a deeper look at the word know. As in the English language, the word know in the Greek (the original language of the New Testament) and Hebrew (the original language of the Old Testament) spans a wide range of meanings. Just as knowing a person casually cannot compare to the knowledge (or knowing) you have of a spouse, family member, or dear friend, so it is in the Bible with the word know.

In Philippians 3:8, when Paul said, "What is more, I consider everything a loss compared to the surpassing greatness of knowing Christ Jesus my Lord," he used the Greek word gnosis, which means knowledge gleaned from first-hand (personal) experience, connecting theory to application through direct relationship.[2] Think back to what Paul told us about himself in Philippians 3:4–7. He was loaded with head knowledge and accomplishments, but it was "a loss" or "rubbish" compared to the first-hand, personal experience of Jesus through a direct relationship.

Paul continued in 3:12–14 to say that he hadn't arrived (my translation), but he "presses on to take hold of that for which Christ Jesus took hold of me." The "that" Paul is talking about is found in 3:10: "I want to know Christ and the power of His resurrection and the fellowship of sharing in His suffering, becoming like Him in His death." Paul deeply desired and pursued intimacy with God.

Are you, like Paul, pressing on to "take hold of that for which Christ Jesus took hold of you" (intimacy), or have you gotten sidetracked at a water station? Reread Philippians 3, and then use the following space to share with God your thoughts about the priority pursuing intimacy with Him has in your life. Talk to Him about any water stations in your life. "Draw near to God and He will draw near to you" (James 4:8).

No matter where you are in your journey right now, God desires to take you further and walk with you into ever-increasing intimacy. Paul forgot his past and pressed on for the future. May we eagerly do the same!

Day 3
Jesus Prayed You Would Have It

At the age of six at a Backyard Bible Club, I prayed what many call the sinner's prayer. It was explained to me that my sin separated me from God, but through Jesus my sins could be forgiven. I could spend eternity with Jesus and God in heaven if I would invite Him into my life. It was a deal that, even at a young age, I couldn't pass up.

The scope of the explanation given to me has thankfully been expanded during the years since, but the questions still remain: What are we getting, and what are we giving? Do we really understand eternal life?

Look up the following passages, and record what Jesus says about eternal life:

John 3:14–16

John 5:39–40

John 17:2–3

God granted Jesus the authority to give eternal life to all people who believe in Him as Savior. Eternal life is often viewed only as the life Christians will have in heaven after their death on this earth. For a more accurate and thorough understanding, consider the Greek definitions for the words eternal and life:

Eternal (Aionios): "Eternal, perpetual. When referring to eternal life, it means the life which is God's and hence is not affected by the limitations of time, but not merely as life that is eternal in duration but primarily something different from the life of natural man, i.e., the life of God."[3]

Life (Zoe): "The fullness of life. When paired with eternal, it is the very life of God of which believers are made partakers."[4]

Taking this definition, rewrite the following passages, inputting "the life of God in them and unending years with Him" in place of eternal life.
John 3:14–16

John 17:1–3

This is intimacy; this is oneness. It is the very life of God in us! This is what we get, but what is our part? Let's call it the divine exchange. We get the life of God in us and unending years with Him in exchange for our lives. Jesus called our part repentance. At the beginning of Jesus' public ministry, Matthew 4:17 tells us, "From this time on Jesus began to preach, "Repent, for the kingdom of heaven is near."

To repent is to have a change of mind. "The (Greek) word metanoeo denotes a change of mind. In terms of salvation (or conversion), repentance denotes a turning away from unbelief, mistrust, and rebellion against God and towards complete reliance upon His forgiveness and favor on account of Christ."[5]

List the three words in the definition that describe what those with sincere repentance turn away from:

What do they turn toward?

Those with sincere repentance are professing to believe, trust, and submit to God. Believing God, trusting God, and submitting to God are part of our journey. They manifest in our lives as we journey with Him in a relationship of intimacy.

> *The Divine Exchange - the life of God in us and unending years with Him in exchange for our life.*

For week 1, it is important to consider a few passages of Scripture that help us understand the heart and resulting life of the truly repentant and why Scripture says that some who think they are saved are not. Put into your own words the warnings given in the following Scriptures:

Matthew 7:17–23 (Note: fruit includes believing, trusting, and submitting to God.)

James 2:19

Now record the words of Jesus in Luke 9:23–24 concerning the actions of those with true repentance:

Many people believe in Jesus, but it's agreeing to take Him at His Word (believe Him), trusting Him with your life, and submitting your will and your ways for Him to live through you—His life for your life—that constitutes the true repentance that brings salvation. In doing this, we accept Him not only as Savior but also as our Lord.

The Full Invitation

You know He's your Savior, but have you submitted to Him as Lord? Summarize the following Scriptures, and record how they apply to you:

Romans 10:9

Galatians 2:20–21

Do we submit fully to His Lordship immediately or perfectly? No, that's all part of the journey of intimacy. Though we may lose our lives, we will gain eternal life—the life of God in us and unending years with Him. It is this that Jesus prayed you would have in John 17:1–3. The word know in verse 3 is from the same root word as the word knowing used by Paul in Philippians 3:8, but this Greek word (*ginosko*) focuses on the knowing being obtained by ongoing exposure and experience. Jesus professed that all those who receive Him as Savior and Lord would walk into the fullness of eternal life—the life of God in them—by knowing God more and more through ongoing exposure and experience.

Those with a sincere repentance are professing to believe, trust and submit to God.

This was Jesus' prayer on the night before His crucifixion. Will you pause now to praise and worship the One who loves and pursues you so much?

Day 4
The Path of Life

King David served as Israel's second king. In God's sovereign plan, David was chosen from among the sons of Jesse. He was the youngest, a shepherd boy, unassuming and by societal standards undeserving, but a man who would give his heart, his ways, and even his days to Almighty God. Scripture deems him "a man after God's own heart" (1 Sam. 13:14). David was not a perfect man, nor was he without great trials, yet he was a man of great joy. He enjoyed great intimacy with God and understood and sought his journey with Him. David is a man from whom we can learn much.

Our focus for today is on Psalm 16, a poem written by King David. Read Psalm 16, and record your insights into whom God was to David. For example, in Psalm 16:1, God was David's refuge. He was his refuge, his Lord, his cup and portion, his counselor, his security, and his source of gladness.

Reread your list, and ponder the depths of David's relationship with God. Are there aspects of this relationship you would like to see in your own life? List them below:

For all you listed, there is great hope! God established our lives to be a journey. David called it a "path of life" in verse 16. It is on this journey that David walked, and now we may walk into an ever-deepening, ever-growing relationship with God and receive those things we listed above.

Let's dissect the first part of Psalm 16:11: "You have made known to me the path of life." Recall our study of the word know from day 3. Old Testament words have a Hebrew origin. The Hebrew for "made known" is yada. Its meaning extends to both God causing us to know and understand as well as God making Himself known to us. As in the New Testament, it is a word signifying intimacy because yada is also used to mean sexual intercourse.[6]

Path in Hebrew is orach, and it has a two-fold meaning as well: a way of living but also the literal journey (places, events) we travel and experience in living. Orach refers to God's way of righteousness and the paths we can choose—one leading to life and one leading to death.[7]

David found through his intimate relationship with God (God making himself known to David) that He also revealed to him the way to live and the decisions he should make, often referred to by David as "the way he should go." This resulted in David having life—the life that is true life: "joy in Your presence and eternal pleasures at Your right hand."

The word life in Deuteronomy 30:15–20 is used in the same way as "path of life" in Psalm 16:11. What insight into our path of life or journey do you glean from Deuteronomy 30:18–20? What is available to you if you choose the path of life?

Do you see that such life is not obtained passively? Are there choices you need to make? Record your thoughts below:

Second Timothy 3:16 says that all Scripture is God breathed. Though Psalm 16 was penned by David, it is still God's Word to you. Write your thoughts to God after each verse of Psalm 16 below:

Psalm 16 (AMP)

1. Keep and protect me, O God, for in You I have found refuge, and in You do I put my trust and hide myself.

2. I say to the Lord, You are my Lord; I have no good beside or beyond You.

3. As for the godly (the saints) who are in the land, they are the excellent, the noble, and the glorious, in whom is all my delight.

4. Their sorrows shall be multiplied who choose another god; their drink offerings of blood I will not offer or take their names upon my lips.

5. The Lord is my chosen and assigned portion, my cup; You hold and maintain my lot.

6. The boundary lines have fallen for me in pleasant places; yes, I have a good heritage.

7. I will bless the Lord, Who has given me counsel; yes, my heart instructs me in the night seasons.

8. I have set the Lord continually before me; because He is at my right hand, I shall not be moved.

9. Therefore my heart is glad and my glory [my inner self] rejoices; my body too shall rest and confidently dwell in safety,

10. For You will not abandon me to Sheol (the place of the dead), neither will You suffer Your holy one [Holy One] to see corruption.

11. You will show me the path of life; in Your presence is fullness of joy, at Your right hand there are pleasures forevermore.

Day 5
Times and Places

I'm excited about the passage of Scripture that will close out our first week of the study. It illustrates the specific and intentional journey God designed for each of us, and in it we see His desire for us to seek Him and reach out for Him.

To begin today's study, please read Acts 17:16–28.

During his first of three missionary journeys, Paul visited (among other cities) Thessalonica and Berea before coming to our passage of Scripture in which he is in Athens. The gospel message was well received in Berea but not in Thessalonica. It was the Jews from Thessalonica who came to stir things up in Berea who caused Paul to leave two of his co-laborers in the gospel, Timothy and Silas, and go ahead of them to Athens. Upon arriving in Athens, Paul was confronted with a society laden with multiple gods.

When Paul arrived at Athens in the province of Achaia, he came to an anomaly. Though its population was no more than ten thousand and it had been reduced to poverty and submission by its war with Rome (146 B.C.), it was granted the status of a free city in view of its illustrious past. "Accordingly, although the time of her greatest glory was gone forever, Athens could still boast of her right to be called a great center of philosophy, architecture, and art"[8]—and, we might add, religion. In fact, what assaulted Paul's spirit was the ubiquitous idolatry. Guarding the entrance to houses and shrines was a square pillar with the head of Hermes, the god of roads, gateways and the marketplace. What Paul met in Athens was "a forest of idols."

With a broken heart and righteous anger, Paul went into the synagogues first—his usual approach—and then to the marketplace. His plea came in such a manner that he boldly spoke the truth but was culturally relevant to those who so desperately need to hear and accept the gospel message. He drew their attention (v. 23) to an altar he saw marked "to an unknown god" and said to them, "Now what you worship as something unknown I am going to proclaim to you." And proclaim he did—and he does so for us also!

Record your insights into:
The greatness of God (vv. 24–26a)

His intentional structuring of your life (v.26)

His desired result is for you to walk on the path / in the journey He designed for you (vv. 27–28).

The God who made the world and everything in it—the God who needs nothing and who gives life to all men—this God determined the exact times and the exact places where you would live. He did this so you would seek Him and perhaps reach out for Him and find Him. He desires that you would live in Him, move in Him, and have your being in Him. It's the divine exchange; you give up your life to gain His life. Praise be to the Lord God Almighty who loves us so much that He went to such great lengths to pursue a relationship with us!

Take a few minutes before proceeding, and ponder this great love. Consider expressing your thoughts to God in the space below:

"So that you would seek Him and perhaps reach out for Him and find Him."
Acts 17:27

Conclusion

Our lives are designed to be a journey in intimacy with God. That's the main event, and out of it the rest of life should flow. Where we have once pursued other things, knowing and loving God should become our number-one pursuit. Anything we choose to give up will be of no comparison to the gift and subsequent joy of knowing how much God loves us, understanding how He sees us, and walking in all He wants to share with us.

David understood many things about this journey he calls "the path of life." Mainly, God was the ultimate cup and portion to be obtained. Get God, and you have life. David also knew that more of the life of God in us comes as we walk with God on the specific path designed for us. On this path, David had joy and found pleasure. But God—not joy, not pleasure, not peace, not comfort, not knowledge, not status—was what he pursued. David got it. David knew that life's ultimate joy is intimacy with God. May this truth become real to us!

I keep asking that the God of our Lord Jesus Christ, the glorious Father, may give you the Spirit of wisdom and revelation, so that you may know Him better. (Eph. 1:17)

Notes

Week 2
God's Presence

Here I am! I stand at the door and knock. If anyone hears my voice and opens the door I will come in and eat with him and he with Me. —Revelation 3:20

Day 1
Here I Am!

Revelation 3:20 reads a little like a dinner invitation:

You are cordially invited to dine with the King of kings and Lord of lords.
Date: Every day
Time: All the time
Place: Where you live and move and have your being.
Please RSVP by: opening the door and letting Him in.

What if a political dignitary or famous actor were to send you an invitation for dinner? Wouldn't you respond quickly, tell friends and family, plan what you would wear, and leave early to make sure you arrived on time? Upon arrival, would you talk about yourself, or would you sit somewhat in awe, hesitant to speak, and aside from trying to hide your nervousness, focus your attention fully on your host?

Should we respond to Jesus' invitation to come into His presence—to eat with Him and He with us—with any less excitement, awe, and desire? Have you responded to Jesus' invitation with less excitement, awe, and desire? Record your thoughts below:

In His quest for intimacy with mankind, God has revealed His presence to man in different ways.
Read and record your thoughts on the following passages:
Psalm 139:7–18; 51:11–12; 16:11

What did David say about God's presence?

How did David feel about God's presence?

Exodus 33:7–23; 13:20–22 (Note: "face" in Hebrew is panch and is also a word for presence.)[1]

How did Moses experience God's presence?

How did Moses feel about God's presence?

Can you recall ways you have experienced God's presence? If so, what feelings did the experience cause in you?

To seek the presence of God is not to seek to get it, for we already have it. Jesus says, "Here I am." What we are seeking is to recognize and respond to Him. Some people are fearful of it, while others simply don't see the importance of taking the time for it. If your answer to the

"Where can I go from your presence?"
Psalm 139:7

question above is no, I can fully relate to you. A part of my spiritual journey was that I didn't think God wanted to reveal Himself to me. I was wrong, and if you think like I did, so are you!

Share with God your thoughts about His presence. Ask God to enable you to seek, recognize, and respond to His presence.

Day 2
I Stand at the Door and Knock

God asks for permission to come into your life and to live His life in you. But not all people give that permission. Adam and Eve knew the presence of God as no one has except Jesus. Unhindered by sin, God and man were in perfect union, living as God designed and desired us to live. Yet such a union was not forced upon them without their choice.

Read Genesis 3:1–12. Adam and Eve once enjoyed intimate fellowship with God:
What changed?

Why did it change?

Who changed?

God previously told them (Gen. 2:15–17) they could eat of every tree in the garden of Eden except the Tree of the Knowledge of Good and Evil, for if they ate of it they would die. Satan, in the form of a serpent (see Rev. 12:9), convinced them they would not die—but they did. God did not mean an immediate physical death, though their bodies would now deteriorate physically. He meant a spiritual death, the death of eternal life, as we studied last week, as well as the death of

To seek the presence of God is not to seek to get it, for we already have it.

the perfect union they had enjoyed. They once had known incredible fellowship with God, but they now ran and hid from Him.

But God Kept Knocking

Adam and Eve's choice was not the end of God's pursuit of intimacy with man. From the beginning, God had a plan: Jesus. Though the fulfillment of that plan was not immediate, God's knocking never ceased as He continually called the people to turn to Him and seek Him. Jeremiah 29 contains a letter from God as spoken through the prophet Jeremiah to the Israelite exiles in Babylon. It's a letter of hope and promise to this specific group of people at a specific time. While we must be careful not to take Scriptures out of context, there's much we can learn about the ways and will of God from it.

Read Jeremiah 29:10–14. Summarize verse 11:

Most translations begin verse 12 with the word *then*. It's used as the phrase "so that" was used in Acts 17:27, which we studied last week. What was God's hoped-for outcome from the plans He had for them?

After doing some research on the Hebrew meaning of some key words, I am cautiously taking the liberty to personalize this passage. It is quite beautiful: "I sit around and simply think of you. In My thinking of you, floods of creative imaginations and ideas come to My mind, and I plan them for your life. I plan them in hopes that you will seek Me so I can give them to you. But mostly I plan them so you will seek Me and find Me so you can be with Me and know My love for you."

They had seventy years to think about this invitation. No matter what their response, God would keep knocking as He still waits at the door until all who will come are ready. Before ending today's study, reflect back on the ways in which God revealed Himself to people in the Old Testament. Think about those who longed for it and those who hid from it. What can you learn from them about seeking God's presence? Record your thoughts below:

"Here I am! I stand at the door and knock. If anyone hears My voice and opens the door I will come in and eat with him and he with Me." Revelation 3:20

Day 3
I Will Come In

If anyone opens the door I will come in . . .

From the days of Adam and Eve to the time of Jesus, God's presence was with His people. It was manifested in various ways and would come upon selected people. It was a powerful presence, as we saw in David, who begged God not to take it from him. We also saw it in Moses, who would have rather stayed in a desert than go without God's presence into a land described as "flowing with milk and honey" (Ex. 3:8).

We live in a new day, under the new covenant, and through Jesus, God's indwelling presence has come into His people. Have you thought about all you were given through Jesus?

Read the following verses, and record your insights under the four headings. (Note: Not all verses will apply to each heading.) John 1:1–2, 14; Colossians 1:15; John 10:25–30, 14:10–11, 17:1–3, 20–26.

A whole new way of knowing God:

A demonstration of oneness with God:

The One given the authority to give us the life of God in us:

> Through Jesus, God's indwelling presence has come in His people.

The One who prayed for our oneness with God:

This oneness would come following Jesus' return to His Father and with the coming of the Holy Spirit. "And you were also included in Christ when you heard the word of truth, the gospel of your salvation. Having believed you were marked in Him with a seal, the promised Holy Spirit" (Eph. 1:13).

For Extra Study

I invite you to read Acts 2. It's a passage in which the apostle Peter seeks to help onlookers understand that the Holy Spirit had just come upon God's people. In it Peter quotes our theme passage from Psalm 16. Record your insights into the context (time and place) Peter quoted the Psalm.

The invitation for Jesus to "come in" was sent worldwide. It's open to anyone. In Revelation 3:14–22, the "anyone" is a group of people Jesus had just disciplined and called indifferent and lukewarm, attributes that caused Him to say, "I am about to spit you out of My mouth." Jesus is calling, asking, knocking, and waiting outside your life to come in and have intimacy with you. It's the intimacy He shared with God while on this earth. It's a worldwide call, but it's also a very personal call to you. When I make John 17:26 personal, it reads, "I have made You known to Judy and will continue to make You known to her so the love You have for me may be in Judy and I myself may be in her." What an amazing invitation is being offered.

Go back to the lists you made and make them personal to you. Use the space below to record your amazing findings:

A whole new way of knowing God:

A demonstration of oneness with God:

The One given the authority to give us the life of God in us:

The One who prayed for our oneness with God:

Day 4
There Is Joy in Your Presence

In last week's lesson, we studied Paul's address to the people in Athens in Acts 17:16–34. Luke, the author of Acts, records that, along with the Jews and the God-fearing Greeks, Paul encountered a group of Epicurean and Stoic philosophers. He shared the gospel, but it made no sense to them: "You are bringing some strange ideas to our ears and we want to know what they mean" (Acts 17:20).

A quick look at their beliefs will teach us a lot. In short, the goal of Epicureanism was pleasure, and they believed it was achieved through the removal of physical pain and mental anxiety. This led them to pursue a very insulated life. They did not embrace learning, culture, and social and political involvement because these could give rise to desires that are difficult to satisfy. This would disturb one's peace of mind, resulting in a loss of feeling pleasure. "Epicureans argue that the path to securing happiness comes by withdrawing from public life and residing with close, like-minded friends."[2]

Stoics believed virtue and wisdom were necessary elements for living a contented and fulfilled life. Therefore they highly valued education as well as participation in various activities. "Regardless of the consequences, one must always perform his/her virtuous duties."[3] Wealth enabled them to perform virtuous acts as well as maintain a level of fitness in their bodies that was essential to their ability to reason and perform their virtuous duties.

Do these mindsets sound familiar? These were the people who could not understand the gospel message presented by Paul. *Have you unknowingly adopted similar mindsets that have prevented you from grasping the words of King David?* Joy comes not from the removal of pain, the performance of virtuous acts, or being highly educated but from being in the presence of God. Sometimes our erroneous mindsets keep us from grasping the fullness of the gospel.

Take a few minutes and consider the question that is italicized above. Ask the Lord to give you insight into any erroneous mindsets you may have, and record your thoughts below:

While researching the beliefs of the Stoics and Epicureans, I stopped to call and wish a friend happy birthday. She shared an experience she had and its spiritual picture of truth that beautifully illustrates the joy we can have in the presence of God. That morning she and her husband went through an automatic car wash—the kind where you sit in your car and are pulled through while water, soap, brushes, and blowing fans buffet your car on the outside. All the while you are untouched on the inside.

In God we are insulated and safe; we can stay dry, protected, and even come out sparkling clean in spite of and often because of the elements coming at us on the outside. This happens because "For you died, and your life is now hidden with Christ in God" (Col. 3:3). To end today, I would like you to spend time talking with God about your search for joy. Have you searched for joy instead of seeking Him? Use this time to "cast all your cares upon Him, because He cares for you" (1 Peter 5:7; Ps. 55:22).

> *Sometimes our erroneous mindsets keep us from grasping the fullness of the gospel.*

Day 5
And Eat with Him and He with Me

A few years ago I attended a Seder—a Jewish feast marking the beginning of Passover—at a local Messianic Jewish temple and got a glimpse into the Hebrew way of dining together. The dinner lasted nearly five hours, but not once was I anxious to leave, even though I only knew two other people there. The evening held great fellowship and sharing as we slowed the pace of our lives to worship God and enjoy one another. The concept of these final words in Revelation 3:20 would have been more widely understood during the times they were written as opposed to our fast food, high-speed Internet world.

God wants to be with His people and for us to slow the pace of our lives and come into a full awareness of His presence in us. This will enable us to know and enjoy Him and ultimately have Him live His life through us. This level of intimacy comes from time spent together. From intimacy comes faith, and from faith, God's presence is released—and in His presence is fullness of joy.

God's invitation to intimacy is an invitation to know Him through walking each day in ever-increasing communion with Him. God—not joy or peace or contentment or anything else—is to be our pursuit. Yet I often allow my flesh and the needs I perceive as being so great to consume me. These words recently flowed from my heart: "How long, O Lord, have my happiness, my peace, my joy, and my contentment been my goal? All along my pursuit of them has prevented the obtainment of them."

How about you? What have you been pursuing? I encourage you to stop right now and take time—and if possible, take a significant amount of time—and ask God to reveal to you the things that have usurped Him as your number-one pursuit. If this is a new practice for you, simply find a quiet place (having your Bible, paper, and a pen may be helpful), and approach God with reverence by praising Him for His greatness and thanking Him for His goodness. Go through a time of repentance for any sins He may bring to your mind. Then ask Him,

"For you died, and your life is now hidden with Christ in God."
Colossians 3:3

"Lord, bring to my mind the things I actively pursue more than I seek You." If you desire, use the space below to record your thoughts.

My prayer ended with, "Forsaking all else, I seek you." In that moment, my resolve was so strong. But how is such oneness and intimacy lived out, especially in those times when I don't feel so resolved and truly do not feel empowered by my ever-failing flesh? Thankfully, it is a journey, and God doesn't expect perfection or a quick arrival. But there is a place to start now, and hopefully our journey together through this study will help equip us for the steps that follow.

Get going by writing out prayers from the following verses:
Get Cleaned Up: Use Psalm 51:10–12.

Get Geared Up: Use John 17:3. Tell God you want to know Him—really know Him. Tell Him you want to experience Him in you and through you.

Commit to Keep it Up: Use Acts 17:26–28. Tell God you recognize His plan for you to seek Him and commit to do it, professing the goal of verse 28a.

Go forth in the knowledge that it is "Not by might, nor by power, but by My Spirit, says the LORD Almighty" (Zech. 4:6).

In God's presence is fullness of joy.

Conclusion

My journey in intimacy with God began and has centered largely on the question: Does God really want intimacy with me? As a child, Revelation 3:20 was one of my favorite verses. It delighted and drew me to Jesus. Yet as the years passed, doubts came as to the validity of that verse for me personally.

Your doubts and the distance you may feel from God may come from an entirely different place. Some people fear intimacy with God; others don't see the need for it, don't desire it, or are too busy for it. In the context of Revelation 3:20, Jesus was speaking to a group of believers who He called lukewarm. They had wealth and therefore felt their needs were met, making them largely indifferent to Him. In verse 19, He called them to repent.

Repentance is a change of mind resulting in a change of direction and behavior. I encourage you to identify any lie you have believed and talk to God about it, repenting if needed. Repentance is a precious gift because it allows God to change our thinking and align it with His truth. Such repentance will be necessary for you to journey in intimacy with God. Remember, God is standing at your door and knocking.

I keep asking that the God of our Lord Jesus Christ, the glorious Father, may give you the Spirit of wisdom and revelation, so that you may know Him better. (Eph. 1:17)

Notes

Week 3
The Trust Issue

Trust—reliance on the integrity, strength, ability, and surety of a person or thing; to have confident expectation and hope.[1]

Day 1
The Elements of Trust

I imagine the conversation going something like this:

God: Do you trust Me?
      Me: Of course I trust You, Lord.
            God: Then why are you anxious?

God: Do you trust Me?
      Me: Of course I trust You.
            God: Then where is your peace?

God: Do you trust Me?

Me: Why wouldn't I trust You?

God: That's what I'd like you to tell Me.

Why wouldn't we trust God? Maybe the question is better asked, why don't we? This week we're going to examine what I am calling the trust issue. We children of God, having already received our salvation by faith, struggle to trust God in the everyday affairs of this life. We believe He loved us enough to send Jesus to die for us. We believe He has the power that raised Jesus back to life. So why aren't such love and power more than we need to firmly believe in the reliability, truth, character, ability, and strength of God and His Word, enabling us to depend on Him for all future needs?

Before reading further, stop and ask God to use this week to reveal any areas in which you are not trusting Him, as well as the reasons why. Record your prayer below:

Trust is inseparably linked to two other words: belief and faith. In the New Testament, the same Greek word pistis (pe-stes) is most often used for all three words.[2] In the definition of trust on page 1, the ideas of belief and faith (dependence on something in the future) are clearly stated.

According to Hebrews 11:1–3, what does it look like for you to walk by faith?

Following the example of Hebrews 11:3, list some things, even though they're not seen or you cannot prove them, in which you have faith:

Why does faith in these things sometimes come easier than faith in God, which leads you to trust Him in all things?

> Trust is inseparably linked to two other words: belief and faith.

We were saved through faith in Jesus Christ because we believed. We are called to walk by faith, not only believing in Him but believing everything He says in His Word. In John 6:25, Jesus began a conversation with a group of people who were following Him. They had been impressed by the miracles He had performed, and they wanted to know, "What must we do to do the works God requires?"

Read John 6:25–29, and record Jesus' answer to their question.

In Ephesians 1:15–21, Paul writes to people of faith. What does he pray for them?

What does he say is available to those who believe?

With such importance and power surrounding trust, faith, and belief, we should not be surprised that opposition would come against them. Tomorrow we will look at two obstacles that block our path. To end today, share with God your thoughts about the trust—or lack of trust—you currently have in Him.

"The work of God is this: to believe in the One He has sent." John 6:29

Day 2
Obstacles in Our Path

Whether with a bulldozer or a threshing rod, the way must be cleared for a new road or path to be made. In our journey into intimacy with God, there must be an ongoing clearing of obstacles to faith and belief. These obstacles keep us from knowing God and therefore keep us from trusting Him. We're going to look at two of those obstacles: the obstacle of lies and the obstacle of doing.

The lies go back to the beginning. As far as we can tell, Adam and Eve believed God made them and that He made the plants and animals in the garden and gave them all to them. Through the deception of Satan, they began to doubt God and were ultimately convinced God couldn't be trusted. Read Genesis 3:1–5, and record the three lies spoken by Satan:

Part of clearing our path toward intimacy with God is uncovering lies we've believed about God. In the following passages, great trust in God is expressed, in spite of earthly circumstances. As you look up each passage, prayerfully consider if there is something in you that believes contrary to the truth about God. Record your insights.

Psalm 9:7–10 (Note: When Scripture speaks of the name of God, it is referring to the character of God or the qualities that comprise God.):

Psalm 13:

Psalm 19:7–11:

The Doing Trap

We are a society of doers, often basing our worth on what we do and how much we get done. I've spent a lot of years wondering and asking God what He wanted me to do: what choice He wanted me to make or what place He wanted me to serve. These are good questions, but when my seeking of God becomes a seeking of what to do, I can easily miss the main point—Him!

That is what happened with the people in John 6:25–42. As we read yesterday, their question to Jesus was, "What must we do to do the works God requires?" A society of doers just like us, in their zeal to do, they missed knowing Jesus.

Read John 6:25–42. Record all Jesus said about Himself:

Record what He said about them:

Record (from the words of the people) evidence they did not believe Him:

From 6:28–29, summarize what Jesus was calling them to do. The Amplified Bible text may help expand your answer:

"They then said, What are we to do, that we may [habitually] be working the works of God? What are we to do to carry out what God requires? Jesus replied, This is the work [service] that God seeks of you: that you believe in the One Whom He has sent [that you cleave to, trust, rely on, and have faith in His Messenger]."

Do you feel the great need to resolve any trust issues so you can cleave to, rely on, and fully trust in the One who is always trustworthy? I certainly do!

God is good - all the time. That is His nature!

Day 3
Teachable Moments

God is good. All the time. God is good. All the time.
God is good. All the time. That is His nature!

This chant is regularly spoken by the people of Kenya I have met over the course of four mission trips. The worship leader begins with, "God is good," and then the people shout, "All the time!" These words are not said lightly by those who don't always know if there will be food to eat the next day.

On my most recent trip to Kenya, the words of the chant were not far from my mind as our entire mission team stood on a hillside overlooking the second-largest slum on the continent of Africa, the Kibera slum in Nairobi. Having come on this mission trip not understanding some things in my own life, one question intensified as I looked at the scene in front of me. Is God good all the time?

I know the answer. Yes! I've experienced that answer many, many times. But I wanted to know it afresh. I asked God, "May I see you as my Good Shepherd?"

Our need is God's opportunity. Go back and read John 6:1–15. The people in John 6 needed food, giving God the opportunity to show up in a big way. That day the people had an opportunity, one we are presented with every day: Ask God to meet a need. Wait for Him to meet that need. Know and trust Him in a new way.

Our Need—God's Opportunity

Most of us can supply our basic needs, and we've learned to either satisfy or quench our emotional needs by self-initiated means. (A dear friend once told me that movies were my drug of choice. She was right!) Will you give God the opportunity to meet a need you are feeling right now? On that day in Kenya I did, saying: "God, I'm not going to fix this today. I feel sad, and I'm coming to You. I ask for two things: for You to lift my heart and for You to reveal to me why I am sad." He did both! I would not have experienced God in such a profound way had I not trusted Him with my need and given Him the opportunity to meet it.

For today, I'd like you to talk to God as you go through Psalm 23. Ask God to meet a need you are feeling right now. Make the passage specific to you: "Lord, I'm asking You to be my Shepherd. You show me the green pasture, and You refresh my soul." Make it specific to you. Talk to Him about all you're feeling and your desire for Him to use your need as His opportunity.

Psalm 23
1. The LORD is my shepherd, I lack nothing.

2. He makes me lie down in green pastures, He leads me beside quiet waters,

3. He refreshes my soul. He guides me along the right paths for His name's sake.

Psalm 23

4. Even though I walk through the darkest valley, I will fear no evil, for You are with me; Your rod and Your staff, they comfort me.

5. You prepare a table before me in the presence of my enemies. You anoint my head with oil; my cup overflows.

6. Surely Your goodness and love will follow me all the days of my life, and I will dwell in the house of the LORD forever.

David, the author of Psalm 23, had also been a shepherd. He fully understood the absolute neediness of sheep. This is what he expressed to God. May we see our neediness as an opportunity for God to reveal Himself to us in new ways.

Day 4
Journey to the Land of All

It's a three-letter word, and God uses it a lot: *all*. We are called to love God with all of our heart, seek God with all of our heart, and trust God with all of our heart. *All* is why intimacy is so important. *All* is why the understanding of our journey is important, for without intimacy and walking in our journey, *all* does not happen.

"Trust in the Lord with all your heart and lean not on your own understanding. In all your ways acknowledge Him, and He will make your paths straight" (Prov. 3:5–6).

The Object of Our Trust
According to Psalm 20:7, what are we to trust in?

"Trust in the Lord with all your heart..."
Proverbs 3:5

As we learned on day 2, when Scripture speaks of the name of God, it is referring to the character of God or the qualities that comprise God—all the qualities that comprise God.

How are we different from "some men?"

Write out a practical example from your life today as to how you can live out the truth in this verse.

David's trust in God was exhibited by the boldness of his expectations of God. Read all of Psalm 20, and make notes below about ways you can begin to pray expectantly and boldly.

Then there was Abraham. Read Romans 4:15–25. Record the principles of faith, belief, and trust that will lead you in your journey to all.

The Problem with Leaning

Even in a physical sense, if the object on which we lean isn't solid, it will not hold us up. It's taken many years, but I do get it: my own understanding of God and His ways is not solid enough on its own to uphold me and direct my path. I recently experienced just this. A decision presented itself that to me was a no brainer, yet when I acted on this no brainer, I had no peace. Instead, the sense in my spirit was to do nothing and simply and fully trust God.

The truth that was revealed from this experience was eye-opening. It came in the meaning of the word acknowledge. I had interpreted acknowledge to mean for me to know the Word of God, know God, and then make a conclusion based on the facts. Steps 1 and 2 are good—know the Word of God and know God—but coming to my own conclusion apart from God is not His plan.

The Hebrew word for acknowledge here is yada. It means to know relationally through experience; specifically in Proverbs 3:6, it means to recognize the claims God has made about Himself. The application is also in Psalm 46:10a: "Be still and know (yada) that I am God." Is there an aspect of your life where you may be leaning on your own understanding and not properly acknowledging God?

Read and then pray Psalm 139:23–24. Record anything God reveals below:

This lesson I recently learned reminded me once again of not only the importance of accurately and intimately knowing God but also of trusting Him to bring His will into my life in ways that may make no sense to me. Following is a poem I believe God placed on my heart during an early-morning time with Him. Thanks to its simplicity, I have never forgotten it:

My ways are not your ways,
My thoughts not your thoughts.
The picture I'm painting doesn't look like you've sought.
But trust Me, just trust Me, and one day you'll see,
your lives will be all I designed them to be.

—Based on Isaiah 55:9

Day 5
Trusting in Christ in Me

When we are trusting God, seeking to live this life by faith, confident of what we hope for and certain of what we do not see (Heb. 11:1), and as we do the work of God, believing in Him and also believing Him (John 6:29), we are trusting and living in the power, ability, and resources of Christ who is in us.

Record your insights from Colossians 1:24–27:

> The giving of our all prepares us to receive God's all.

It's a glorious truth: the fullness and the mystery kept hidden for ages and generations are now given to us: Christ in us, the hope of glory.

Often our fear of trusting God stems from our own lack of ability. So many times my pleas to God have sounded something like, "I know You can, but I'll get in the way." Aside from the fact that I was giving myself far too much credit, the truth I was missing was that we are not called to go forth in our own strength. As we continue to identify with Christ's death and resurrection by dying to our own desires and self-governing, we experience greater manifestation of the life of God in us. The goal is that we don't go forth at all but Christ in us goes forth. Then the glory of God can be displayed through us.

With such a glory awaiting us, we do not want to be naive to the consequences of a lack of trust. The Bible speaks often of stewardship. In Matthew 25:21, Jesus is telling a parable to explain a biblical principle and says, "You have been faithful with a few things. I will put you in charge of many things. Come and share your master's happiness." This stewardship principle can be applied to the knowledge of God, which He entrusts to us.

Read Matthew 25:14–30. Explain how this principle would play out if the talent given you is knowledge of God revealed to you by God:

If you didn't do so above, explain how you could put the knowledge to work and gain more.

The giving of our all prepares us to receive God's all. "In all your ways acknowledge Him, and He will make your paths straight." All that God has to give us is on His path for us as we journey through life with Him. On that straight path, we are not deterred by the rough terrain or prevented from receiving all He, as He dreamed and imagined our lives, put on the path. His ways are not our ways and neither are His thoughts our thoughts, but if we will trust Him, He can give us all He has designed for us.

Conclusion

Close this week by pondering the blessings that come to those who trust in the Lord with all their heart. Thanks for working through these trust issues with me.

Blessed is the man who trusts in the LORD, whose confidence is in Him. He will be like a tree planted by the water that sends out its roots by the stream. It does not fear when heat comes; its leaves are always green. It has no worries in a year of drought and never fails to bear fruit. (Jer. 17:7–8) Let us pray this together: "Let the morning bring me word of Your unfailing love, for I have put my trust in You. Show me the way I should go, for to You I entrust my life. (Ps. 143:8)

Notes

Week 4
The Wall of Independence

Day 1
The Potter and the Clay

This is the word that came to Jeremiah from the Lord, "Go down to the potter's house, and there I will give you My message." So I went down to the potter's house and I saw him working at the wheel. But the pot he was shaping from the clay was marred in his hands; so the potter formed it into another pot as seemed best to him. Then the word of the Lord came to me: "O house of Israel, can I not do with you as this potter does?" declares the Lord (Jer. 18:1-6).

A potter labors at his wheel to bring forth a predetermined vessel of loveliness and usefulness. The clay has no vision for itself and only because it lies in the hands of the potter are its true beauty and function brought forth. The clay has no control over itself; it cannot do what the potter can do. How foolish for a lump of clay to resist the forming hand of its potter. Yet how much more foolish is it of the created to resist the Lordship of the Creator?

He Is God! We Are Not.

The role of a lord or sovereign was better understood in other times and cultures than ours today. To those under their reign, obedience wasn't optional. Disobedience was often punishable by death. While citizens often had little control over which kingdom and person ruled over them, we are given a choice to accept Jesus as Savior and Lord or to reject Him and go our own way. We need to note that once that choice for Him is made, His lordship over our lives should be established.

Do we give God the title of Lord but not submit to His rule? Jesus addressed this in Luke 6:46: "Why do you call me 'Lord, Lord' and not do what I say?" The word Jesus used for Lord is kyrios in the Greek, and it means, "He to whom a person or thing belongs, one who has power of deciding, master, lord, owner, possessor."[1] This is a title given to God, the Messiah. The men and women of Jesus' day understood the title. Let us not be like them and fail to surrender to His role.

Stop for a minute and ask yourself a few questions: Do you call Him Lord and not do what He says? If so, why don't you surrender? (This is a loaded question! I encourage you take some time with God to seek the answer.)

We are not alone in our struggle to surrender to God's role as our Lord. Mankind has struggled since the beginning. Satan's third lie to Adam and Eve was that by eating the fruit of the Tree of the Knowledge of Good and Evil, they would be like God. He was enticing them, among other things, with being in control, having power to decide, and being their own master. I think we can call it the clincher lie; it got them.

The nation of Israel struggled also, and it was this struggle of lordship that God brings before them in Jeremiah 18. Reread Jeremiah 18:1–6, and answer the following questions:

What was it that the Lord longed to do with Israel?

"Why do you call me 'Lord, Lord' and not do what I say?" Luke 6:46

How does His longing fit His role as their Lord?

The following two passages include the phrase: "I will be your God." Record your findings about the Lordship of God for the people.

Exodus 6:1–8

Leviticus 26:1–13

Their history would look a lot different if only they would have allowed God to have the role as their Lord, doing with them, as the potter did, "as seemed best to him." It's a sobering thought, especially in light of the lordship we are called to give Him over our lives. Take a few minutes and talk to God about your own struggle to give Him lordship. Record your conversation:

Day 2
The Big Lie

Independent: to be free from outside control, not depending on or influenced by another's authority; thinking or acting for oneself.²

We may think we're good at managing our lives, but Scripture says otherwise. We may strive to obtain independence, but God says we'll never have it. A consequence of it is the erection of a wall between God and you, keeping you from fully knowing Him and walking in intimacy.

All independence from God is sin. All sin is independence from God.

Adam and Eve's hope in eating the fruit of the Tree of the Knowledge of Good and Evil was to be like God, free from outside control, and having no need to depend on or be influenced by God's authority. I don't sense from the Scriptures that it was an act done in anger against God but an act done to the pleasing and betterment of themselves. Maybe what they desired was a little freedom from God's absolute control. A little God, a little me—it sounds like a plan I've often tried to implement. Yet what they obtained was far, far from better. From that point forward, the whole world came under the control of the evil one (1 John 5:19b). Where once God had dominion over them, now sin through the sin nature held that dominion. It was at this point that Adam and Eve lost their intimacy with God.

We are either slaves to sin or slaves to righteousness. The lie that there is a middle ground of independence is as false today as it was in the garden of Eden. This lie is exactly what the evil one used as he tempted Adam and Eve: "For God knows that when you eat of it your eyes will be opened, and you will be like God, knowing good and evil." As a result, there is knowledge of good and evil, where once evil was unknown, but we did not become like God. Instead, the world and all in it came under the control of the evil one.

But God made a way …

Read the passages below and record your findings, taking special note of the words powerless, slaves, mastery, reign, and instruments. This exercise will take a significant amount of time to do thoroughly. Invest the time, and let God open your eyes to truth as He dispels the lie of independence.

Romans 5:6–8, 18–19

> *If we really believe God's ways are higher than ours, His plan greater than ours, then why do we struggle with wanting our own way?*

Our acts of independence invite the influence of the evil one back into our lives. Yet it need not be so. For a child of God, Satan's control has been broken, and according to Romans 5:17, "For if, by the trespass of the one man, death reigned through that one man, how much more will those who receive God's abundant provision of grace and of the gift of righteousness reign in life through the one man, Jesus Christ." This reigning happens "through the one man, Jesus Christ" as we live in dependence upon God.

Praise be to our Lord and Savior Jesus Christ!

Day 3
If We Really Believe ...

Since the early days of our marriage, my husband and I have had many conversations beginning with the phrase: "If we really believe what we say we believe, then why _____?" We've filled in the blank with many different topics and our actions in them. It's a question that deserves repeating and that should continually bring us to consider our actions in light of what we say we believe. Let me make it specific to this lesson: If we really believe God's ways are higher than ours and His plan greater than ours, then why do we struggle with wanting our own way?

We all recognize this is part of the sin nature we are born with, which we are to continually be putting to death. Spend time with a young child and words like "that's mine" and "no" will indicate how deep the self-centered, independent nature runs. Yet we saw yesterday that we have been set free from the power of sin. So what must we do to do the works that God requires? (I hope you recognize this question.) According to Jesus (John 6:29), we must believe.

Taking Knowledge from Head to Heart

How do we take knowledge from our heads to our hearts so it's lived out in our lives? Read Romans 10:16–17, and record your findings:

This verse and the surrounding passage were written concerning the Jewish people, who Isaiah prophesied would not believe, but its principle of truth applies to us: faith comes by hearing the Word of God. However, the passage points out that even those who hear don't always believe.

Read Jesus' parable of the sower in Luke 8:1–15 for one explanation of why.

What are you doing with the Word of God that is being sown into your life?

When you hear the words of God, do you allow Satan to immediately snatch them away?

Do you believe for a while, but when the going gets tough ("a time of testing"), do you fall away?

Does God's Word fall as among thorns because there are so many worries, concerns, pleasures, commitments, or other priorities in your life that you don't take time to nurture it? Or does it fall on a heart not caught in the trap of the three poor soils? Does His Word find that your heart is fertile, well-tilled soil prepared for seed? (Note: God prophesied in Ezekiel 36:26 that He would "give you a new heart and put a new spirit in you; I will remove from you your heart of stone and give you a heart of flesh.") Jesus says the first group of hearers is not saved. Scholars differ on the salvation of the second group, but for our consideration we should prayerfully look at the second and third types of soil, for it is here that the wall of independence is often erected. What changes do you need to make in your life for the Word of God to fall on fertile soil, allowing it to move from your ears and head to your heart?

> ...it's part of our ongoing struggle to submit to His plans, His ways.
>
> it and by perserverance produce a crop."
> Luke 8:15

44

Day 4
Be Careful What You Ask For

Be careful what you ask for; you just might get it. It's something we've likely all encountered at some point. We want something, we go after something, we get something, but what we end up with is not what we wanted at all. Sometimes we want something God wants us to have, but we go about getting it our way. For God's people, then and now, it's part of our ongoing struggle to submit to His plans and His ways. It comes in many forms: we don't wait for His timing; we don't go through the hard path (because how could that be God's will for me?); we move ahead of God (ahead of God's provision and protection).

Isaiah 30 centers on a time in Israel's history when she attempted to make an alliance with Egypt in hopes of gaining Egypt's assistance in their fight against a very strong and threatening Assyrian empire. Though Egypt's power was greatly waning at that time, in Israel's search for peaceful borders, she turned to Egypt for salvation and strength instead of turning to and depending on God. Read Isaiah 30:1–18. In answering the following questions, seek to apply it to your modern-day life.

From 30:1–2, record some of the actions taken by Israel:

From 30:3–5, record what the outcome was prophesied to be:

Isaiah 30:6–7 describes the land through which they would pass on their way to Egypt. (Note: Isaiah calls Egypt by the name Rahab.) What would they encounter on their journey?

> "In all
> your ways
> acknowledge
> Him and He
> will make your
> paths straight."
> Proverbs 3:6

How did Isaiah describe the hearts of the people in 30:8–11?

What were the consequences going to be according to 30:12–15?

In verse 15, God reveals His answer to their problem. Meditate on this passage, and then write your insights below.

From 30:16–17, what does God, through the prophet Isaiah, foretell will happen because they chose to do it their way?

Last week's passage from Proverbs 3:6 comes to my mind: "In all your ways acknowledge Him and He will make your paths straight." Their path could have been so much straighter—free from unnecessary and devastating obstacles they were going to face and free from defeat—for He would have delivered them. But in their independence, they would have none of it.

May we learn from the mistakes of those in the past! Do you need to confess the sin of independence? Isaiah 30:18 speaks to the character of God—the God of Israel and the God of all of us who have been grafted in. May its words bless you.

And therefore the Lord [earnestly] waits [expecting, looking, and longing] to be gracious to you; and therefore He lifts Himself up, that He may have mercy on you and show loving-kindness to you. For the Lord is a God of justice. Blessed (happy, fortunate, to be envied) are all those who [earnestly] wait for Him, who expect and look and long for Him [for His victory, His favor, His love, His peace, His joy, and His matchless, unbroken companionship]! (Isa. 30:18 AMP)

Day 5
The Freedom of Dependence

I have tended to worry about things over which I have no control (which is most things) and inwardly grumble about things I know I have to do. In doing so, I take on burdens and weight that I was never meant to carry. Can you relate? During a recent time of fretting, the freedom I could have through choosing to be dependent on God became so clear from the pages of Scripture. It came in four words:

Come   **Cast**   **Cling**   **Carried**

Record your insights from the following passages, taking special note of the action words listed above:

Matthew 11:28–30

1 Peter 5:6–7

Psalm 63:1–8. Include a description of David's heart for God (vv.1–7).

Exodus 19:3–8

I find it helpful to use my imagination to picture myself coming to Jesus. I picture Him and me walking toward Him (come). When I arrive in front of Him, I take the burdens on my heart and lay them at His feet (cast). Then I wrap my arms around Him (cling). In doing this, I now see myself being carried.

There is an order to this. I must first come. Without coming, I can't cast my cares on Jesus. I can fling them in the air, thinking I'm letting go, but they only clutter the matter and I end up picking them back up later. Then I must cast, for with hands full of worries, I cannot cling. Note that I did not place them in Jesus' hands, for He has already overcome all of my circumstances, and He simply wants me to cast them so that He can carry me.

If you are comfortable, I encourage you to try this. Take the burden on your heart and come, cast, cling, and be carried by Jesus.

Come
Cast
Cling
Be Carried

Conclusion

The content has been weighty this week because living independent of God brings dire consequences. The deception of being our own gods and in control of our lives goes back to the garden of Eden. In addition, we live in a world designed to function through independence and a flesh that is mightily drawn to it. In these, the battle can fiercely rage against depending on God.

Independence could also be described as pride, and God's Word about pride is clear: "God opposes [fights against] the proud, but He gives grace to the humble" (James 4:6). The nation of Israel in Isaiah 30 is a clear example of this.

But God is faithful! He will not let you be tempted beyond what you can bear, and when you are tempted, He will provide a way to hold up under it (1 Cor. 10:13). Our role is to humble ourselves under God's mighty hand by humbling our will, humbling our ways, and surrendering to His ways. In doing so, He can lift us up (James 4:10), and considering He is God, His lifting will be amazing!

Our best weapon against independence is to pursue God above all else, and the journey in that is where we'll pick up next week. Until then, ponder and pray for the heart of David seen in Psalm 63. David wrote the psalm during a time in a dry, waterless wilderness of Judah. Since he was being pursued by enemies, he was away from the ark of the covenant, his formal place of worship. Yet God was still very near and very real to him. David understood something we'd be wise to grasp: it's a privilege to be dependent on God.

O God, You are my God, earnestly I seek You; my soul thirsts for You, my body longs for You, in a dry and weary land where there is no water. I have seen You in the sanctuary and beheld Your power and Your glory. Because Your love is better than life, my lips will glorify You. I will praise You as long as I live, and in Your name I will lift up my hands. My soul will be satisfied as with the richest of foods; with singing lips my mouth will praise You. On my bed I remember You; I think of You through the watches of the night. Because You are my help, I sing in the shadow of Your wings. My soul clings to You; Your right hand upholds me. (Ps. 63:1–8)

I pray God will firmly plant His words upon your heart; may they never be snatched again.

> It's a privilege to be dependent on God.

Notes

Week 5
Praise! Praise! Praise!

Praise: to extol, exalt, glorify; the offering of grateful homage as an act of worship.
The joyful thanking and adoring of God, the celebration of His goodness and grace.
An act rightfully due God alone.[1]

Day 1
Praise: Will You Do It?

"It Hardly Felt Like a Time to Praise Him" was the title of an article I ran across many years ago. It was written by a woman in difficult circumstances, including the end of a longtime marriage at her husband's request, followed by a diagnosis of cancer. While sharing her struggles with a Christian friend, she was presented with what seemed an odd and almost insensitive challenge: to spend twenty minutes a day for two weeks praising God. Though she felt void of anything to be thankful for and lacked any desire of her own to praise, she accepted the challenge with a "What have I got to lose?" attitude.

Two weeks turned into months, and the transformation in her was remarkable. She found joy, peace came, and hope returned, though her circumstances remained the same. Such, the article concluded, is the power of praise. This is the power of praising God! "Let everything that has breath praise the Lord" (Ps. 150:6).

The Bible is clear in its command for us to praise God. The entire book of Psalms is devoted to it. The command is not exclusive to happy times or times when we feel like praising God. In the book of Psalms, the praises range from emotions of ecstatic delight to earnest pleading and even to deep despair. Yet in them all the command remains, "Let everything that has breath praise the Lord."

How do you feel about praising God right now in your circumstances? Do you feel like this woman did—void of anything to be thankful for? Or are you in a season of fruitfulness, making it easy to praise Him? In whichever place you find yourself, will you undergo the twenty minutes a day praise challenge?

Psalm 100 will be our guide.

"Shout for joy to the LORD, all the earth. Worship the LORD with gladness; come before Him with joyful songs. Know that the LORD is God. It is He who made us, and we are His; we are His people, the sheep of His pasture. Enter His gates with thanksgiving and His courts with praise; give thanks to Him and praise His name. For the LORD is good and His love endures forever; His faithfulness continues through all generations."

The challenge is for your praise of God to come in two ways. First, start by giving thanks to God for the things He does and provides for you. As I have taken on this challenge, there are days when thanksgiving flows easily, and there have been days when, with a burdened heart, I thank God for seemingly insignificant things. In it all, I enter His gate (Ps. 100:4), much like the priests in the Old Testament did as they prepared to serve in the tabernacle.

Praising God for who He is comes next. I see this as an entering of His court (Psalm 100:4), including His inner court, the Holy of Holies, where only the high priest was allowed to enter once a year. In the New Testament we are called a royal priesthood (1 Peter 2:9), and we may enter into the Holy of Holies of God's presence at any time. We do so through the holy act of praise.

"Let everything
that has
breath praise
the Lord."
Psalm 150:6

We need not rush into His presence so we can tell Him our needs. The purpose of coming into the inner courts with praise is to prepare our hearts to come into His presence. It doesn't have to be formal but a reverent act of humility.

To begin your time of praise today, I encourage you to read 1 Chronicles 16:7–36. David challenges the people to give thanks and praise to God. He gives examples of how to praise (singing), what you can praise Him for (His wonders and miracles), and a challenge to praise God for who He is (great, worthy). Let Him guide you as you begin this twenty minutes a day praise challenge.

Use the following space to record your thanksgiving and praise. In the beginning, it may help to set a timer so you are not distracted by watching the clock.

Day 1 Praises:

"You are a chosen people, a royal priesthood, a holy nation, a people belonging to God that you may declare the praises of Him who called you out of darkness into His wonderful light."
1 Peter 2:9-10

Day 2
Praise Lights Our Path

We praise God foremost because He alone is worthy of all our praise. Yet it is for our benefit that God has ordained His people to praise Him, for our God "is not served by human hands, as if He needed anything" (Acts 17:25).

As I am intentional to praise God according to the truth in His Word, one thing happens without fail: my awareness of God and His grace gets bigger, and the oppression of my circumstances gets smaller. I have found the lyrics of the song to be true every time: "Turn your eyes upon Jesus, look full in His wonderful face, and the things of earth will grow strangely dim in the light of His glory and grace."[2]

To put it bluntly, praising God keeps me from moaning about me. Thanking God for what He's done and praising Him for who He is sheds the light of truth on our circumstances. Otherwise our grumbling may lead us off our path of intimacy. It reminds us of who God is and His faithful track record in the past. Praise can take us from being defeated by what our eyes see to trusting in faith according to who God is and what He promises to do. This is because we are thinking on what is true.

Is there an area in your life where you've found yourself moaning or grumbling? Will you let the praise challenge shed some light there and turn your grumbling words into praise? Consider using the following words of David in Psalm 145 to begin your twenty minutes of praise, professing the truth of God's care over all your circumstances. Record your praise on the following page:

"The Lord is faithful to all His promises and loving toward all He has made. The Lord upholds all those who fall and lifts up all who are bowed down. The eyes of all look to You, and You give them their food at the proper time. You open your hand and satisfy the desires of every living thing." (Ps. 145:13–16)

Praising God keeps me from moaning about me.

Day 2 Praises:

"The Lord is faithful to all His promises and loving toward all He has made."
Psalm 145:13

Day 3
Praise: Dispels Darkness

Of the 150 Psalms, 73 are attributed to David, and many of them are psalms cried out in distress. Praise not only sheds light on our path, but it also serves as a tool of warfare for our journey. Psalm 8:1–2 speaks of the power of praise ordained by God.

O LORD, our Lord, how majestic is Your name in all the earth. You have set Your glory above the heavens. From the lips of children and infants You have ordained praise because of Your enemies, to silence the foe and avenger.

God led the nation of Israel to use praise in warfare. The walls of Jericho came down with a trumpet blast and a loud shout (Josh. 6:1–21). Jehoshaphat and the men of Judah defeated a great multitude coming against them by singing and praising God (2 Chron. 20:1–30). I encourage you to read these amazing stories. Note that the praise came before the victory.

Praise is also one avenue of taking our thoughts captive and making them obedient to the knowledge of God. This is one of the divine weapons we are given to fight with (2 Cor.10:4–6).

David often found himself in distressing circumstances in which he poured his heart out honestly to God. Yet as Psalm 13 shows, after the sharing of his heart, David ends with truth, trust in God's unfailing love, and praise for God's salvation and goodness toward him.

Read Psalm 13, and in your twenty minutes of praise, consider pouring out any burden on your heart, but end with your own psalm of praise.

How long, LORD? Will You forget me forever? How long will You hide Your face from me? How long must I wrestle with my thoughts and day after day have sorrow in my heart? How long will my enemy triumph over me? Look on me and answer, LORD my God. Give light to my eyes, or I will sleep in death, and my enemy will say, "I have overcome him," and my foes will rejoice when I fall. But I trust in Your unfailing love; my heart rejoices in Your salvation. (Ps. 13)

> Praise not only sheds light on our path, but it serves as a tool of warfare for our journey.

Day 3 Praises:

Day 4
Praise: Just Share It

Have you ever come across something too good to keep to yourself? Good news is like that: a sale at the mall; an amazing book; a wonderful movie. Some news is so good that we just have to share it. How much more should the wonders of our God become like that?

All that You have made will praise You, O Lord; Your saints will extol You. They will tell of the glory of Your kingdom and speak of Your might so that all men may know of Your mighty acts and the glorious splendor of Your kingdom. (Ps. 145:10–11)

Give thanks to the Lord, call on His name; make known among the nations what He has done, and proclaim that His name is exalted. Sing to the Lord, for He has done glorious things, let this be known to all the world. Shout aloud and sing for joy, people of Zion, for great is the Holy One of Israel among you. (Isa. 12:4–6, a prophecy for the nation of Israel)

I recently saw a Christian friend I had not seen in a while. Her words were a testimony of the power of praise when shared publicly. She spoke specifically and sweetly of the faithfulness and kindness of God, all while in the midst of great suffering. As she spoke, it hit me that sincere praise spoken from a thankful heart is not only an act of worship to God but a powerful testimony and gift to the hearer. She inspired me to seek and praise God more.

May a result of our twenty minutes of praise challenge be a heart of such overflowing praise and gratitude that it's so good we just have to share it. At the end of recording today's praises, ask God to give you a heart overflowing with praise and an opportunity to share it.

> ..a thankful heart is not only an act of worship to God, but a powerful testimony and gift to the hearer.

Day 4 Praises:

"Give thanks to the Lord, call on His name; make known among the nations what He has done."
Isaiah 12:4

Day 5
Praise: Keep It Going

> *"Let us continually offer to God a sacrifice of praise."*
> Hebrews 13:15

During His time on earth, Jesus showed us a deeper level of intimacy with God. When the disciples asked Jesus to teach them to pray, He taught them to call God "Father." He also taught the importance of praise, making it the first element of prayer (Matt. 6:9–13).

In John 17:21, Jesus prays that we will be one with the Father, just as He and the Father are one. Such oneness is to be our goal, and there may be no other step we take that will propel us into intimacy more than an ongoing chorus of praise to God. The author of Hebrews spoke of it: "Through Jesus, therefore, let us continually offer to God a sacrifice of praise—the fruit of lips that confess His name" (Heb. 13:15).

It's the will of God: "Be joyful always, pray continually, give thanks in all circumstances, for this is God's will for you in Christ Jesus" (1 Thess. 5:19). It's His will for us, not because He needs our praise but because we need to praise Him! Perhaps the best way to begin is to say thank you to God throughout the day. After your twenty minutes of focused praise, will you seek to talk to God throughout the day simply by saying thank you as you go on your way? Record your praise below and on the following page.

Day 5 Praises:

Conclusion

There's no reason for the challenge to end.

Praise is an act of our will, and it will take practice. It's in the practice of praise that our awe and reverence of God increase, which leads to ever-increasing praise. It can become a beautiful cycle, one that spurs you on to great intimacy with God.

Philippians 2:10–11 states, "At the name of Jesus, every knee will bow, in heaven and on earth and under the earth, and every tongue confess that Jesus Christ is Lord, to the glory of God the Father." We have the privilege of bowing our knees and our hearts now. Will you make praise a daily part of your journey in intimacy with God? If you do, you will find not only your intimacy with God deepening but your trust, dependence, and love for Him increasing as well.

Revelation 4:11 says, You are worthy, our Lord and God, to receive glory and honor and power, for You created all things, and by Your will they were created and have their being.

Let everything that has breath praise the Lord!

"At the name of Jesus every knee will bow..." Philippians 2:10

Notes

Week 6
Knowing All of God

Day 1
An Experiential Knowledge of God

I started thinking about the various roles in which I am known. I'm a wife, mother, mother-in-law and grandmother. I'm a daughter, granddaughter, and daughter-in-law, as well as an aunt and great aunt. I'm a first, second, and third cousin, along with being a niece and great niece. (We marry young and live to an old age in my family.) Those are just the family roles I play. I'm also known as friend, neighbor, customer, and teacher. Though I could tell you about the roles I play, for you to really know me, you would need to be in relationship with me in one or more of those roles. The more roles in which you related to me, the more you would come to know me.

The same is true with God. We can spend years learning about Him, but intimacy will come as we experience Him through relationship in His various roles. The practice of this is what we will seek this week.

Let's begin with a quick review. In week 1, we looked at the meaning of the word know as found in Philippians 3:8 and John 17:3.

"I consider everything a loss compared to the surpassing greatness of knowing Christ Jesus my Lord." (Phil. 3:8)

"Now this is eternal life (the life of God in you and endless years with Him), that they know You, the only true God, and Jesus Christ whom You sent." (John 17:3)

The Greek word for know is gnosis, and it means knowledge gleaned from first-hand experience, connecting theory to application through direct relationship.[1] This direct relationship is what Jesus' death on the cross made possible. It was symbolically portrayed in the temple at the time of His crucifixion: "At that time the curtain of the temple was torn in two from top to bottom" (Matt. 27:51). God removed the veil, and we can now enter into the Holy of Holies directly into His presence.

Such knowledge through seeking God is what Paul shared with the people of Athens in Acts 17:16–28. Though we covered this also in week 1, go back and reread the passage. Then summarize verses 24–28 below:

God determined the times we would live and the exact places where we would live. To consider how detailed His planning might be for you, read and record your insights from Psalm 139:1–18:

God's specific and detailed planning of your life had a purpose: "So that you would seek Him and perhaps reach out for Him and find Him, though He is not far from each one of us" (Acts 17:27). Our reaching out for God results in intimacy from the firsthand experience we will gain as we live and move and have our being in Him. The words "live and move" and the phrase "have our being" describe the breath and movement that are part of sustaining every living creature. The phrase "in Him," however, is what sets apart the follower of Jesus.

> "At that time the curtain of the temple was torn in two from top to bottom."
> Matthew 27:51

When we live, move, and have our being in Him (in Christ), it becomes Christ living and operating in us, the holy mind and energy of Christ pervading and moving in us (Thayer's Lexicon Dictionary).

This application is the same for Galatians 2:19–21, and each use of the word live or lives. Read and then record your insights from this passage:

What did Paul say in Galatians 2:20 that he no longer did?

What does that mean to you and for your life?

The life of living in Him is the oneness Jesus exhibited with the Father while on earth. Jesus set a high standard, one I feel very far from but that I am journeying toward. It's a walk with God, which we will continue to look at and practice in the weeks ahead. For a glimpse, read and record your insights from John 5:19–20, 12:49–50:

> *To experience oneness with God requires practice.*

Day 2
An Opportunity to Know God

The awareness and experience of oneness with God that Scripture describes does not come automatically, even though God is in us. It's something we must practice to become increasingly aware of God's indwelling presence as well as His omnipresence. This is a primary part of our journey into intimacy with God.

Today I'm going to share with you a day where I sought throughout the day, in the various roles I play, to know God better. I purposed to seek Him and to live and move and have my being in Him. Tomorrow it will be your turn!

****

I woke early, feeling burdened as I considered the days ahead and all that needed to be done. My mind turned to earthly solutions. "I know it's nothing for You, God, but it feels like too much for me." I struggled in my time with God this morning. "I'm still carrying the burden. Yet I am filled with desire to want to know You more as I trust You as my God who provides." Desire needed to turn into surrender, for I still didn't have peace.

An opportunity to know God: You are faithful. You have always been faithful, even when I don't feel it.

I texted a Bible verse to a friend in a dire circumstance. She texted back: "Praising God while I wait."

"Oh Lord, how could I so easily forget?" I turned to praising God, and within minutes I moved from dwelling on how much I had to do to how much I am loved by God. As God's love filled my heart, my worries faded; they grew dim in comparison to the light of Christ. Not only were my thoughts replaced by the truth of God's love, but love for others welled up in me.

An opportunity to know God: You speak to me through others. You want me to come into Your presence and be given Your perspective. How much I need Your perspective! You invite me in through praise into the inner court. When you fill me with Your love, I love the things You love and I am able to do all You ask me to do.

Next, I rejoiced and prayed.

After an hour of exercise and coffee now in hand, I thanked God for both—yes, even for exercise and especially for coffee! I drove to make a delivery to a dear friend. We met in a parking lot, and with our cars parked side by side, I delighted in this friendship. It's a gift from God. "God, thank You for Christian sisters and for designing us to be interdependent upon one another."

An opportunity to know God: The vulnerable sharing that goes on in this relationship is just a taste of the ongoing interaction You desire with me and the honesty with which I can come to You.

As I drove away, I marveled that I woke unnecessarily burdened, self-consumed. Yet as I sought to live this day with God, He met me. As my praise of God continued, my heart filled with wonder at the greatness and yet intimate nature of God.

It's only 9:30 a.m.

The day continued. Invitations needed to be mailed. I said prayers for the recipients. Packing needed to be done. I was thankful for the opportunity of this trip.

As I drove to the airport, two verses came to my mind: "Consider it pure joy, my brothers, when you face trials of many kinds" (James 1:2). Yes, where I have tended to grumble, I want to count all things as an opportunity for joy as I live this day with my Lord. "In everything give thanks, for this is God's will for you in Christ Jesus" (1 Thess. 5:18). Yes God, I will.

An opportunity to know God: You are the God who, through Your Holy Spirit, reminds us of things You have said (John 14:26). Your words are not to be taken lightly. (This is an insight I will later wish I had heeded.)

At the airport, I observed a mother holding her little boy. She held him so tenderly as he talked to her. I didn't come close to understanding his speech, but she did and answered him. Both his parents took care of all the details for going through airport security. He sat contentedly on his mother's hip.

An opportunity to know God: This is a picture of how You hold me, of how You look at me. You understand my words even when I can't express them clearly because You know my every thought. If I will let You, You will take care of all my needs.

On the flight, I sat next to a woman named Bernice. A quick comment I made about the magazine she was reading led to a deeper discussion. She had just buried her fifty-four-year-old daughter, a cancer victim. "She's so stoic. Lord, what strength she displays. How can I be You to her? Yes, I'll ask if I can pray for her." I asked Bernice if I could pray for her, thinking she'd say yes and I would pray later. Instead, this woman who just moments ago spoke almost without any emotion about her daughter's death plunged her head on my shoulder, grabbed onto my arm, and waited for me to pray.

An opportunity to know God: "We all need You, Lord. Deep down, all people need You, a need You placed in us so we would seek You. I see afresh how much You want us to seek You. I see afresh how close You always are. May Bernice seek You; may I seek You more. Help me again to die to my own thoughts and agendas."

As I arrived at my destination in Washington, D.C. I was full of the energy this city gives me. So much is always going on there. Yet I was reminded, "You set the exact times and places I would live so that I would seek You, and You've only given me Washington, D.C. for short-term visits." I laughed but again was reminded that I have another opportunity to know God: "You said it's possible to be content in all circumstances, and my contentment is not about my location; it's about living and moving and having my being in You. This is possible in all circumstances. Yes, in all things Lord, I can be content (Phil. 4:12–13)."

While getting ready for a dinner with friends, the bad news came like a crushing weight. The friend in dire circumstances had just received devastating news. I found it hard to breathe. I didn't want to feel. I didn't want to conceive what she must be feeling. I wanted to fall back into the old habit of shutting it all out, including God.

An opportunity to know God: I'm not sure I want to know God at this moment, and I'm ashamed I feel that way. I don't want to deal with my feelings of disappointment, disillusionment, and fear; but for me to live and move and have my being in God, I will have to. I will take all of these feelings to God. He is enough. Again I will ask myself, will I choose to trust that God is good all the time? Will I choose to trust Him no matter what? (This did not happen quickly.)

I look back at the even greater opportunities to know God: He's the God who sought to prepare me by reminding me to "consider it all pure joy" and "to give thanks in everything." He had reminded me that it is possible for people to "be content in all circumstances," for as the passage continues, "we can do all things through Him who gives us strength" (Phil. 4:13). He'd shown me, just that morning, the power that praising Him has to give me His perspective.

Praise first returned as I simply rewrote words from the Psalms. I longed for the words to become my own, for at first they were not. Yet in time I was once again living and moving and having my being in Him, though the heaviness remained.

****

There are multitudes of ways from the events of this one day in which I had the opportunity to intimately know God through an interactive and experiential relationship. It came by seeking to live and move and have my being in Him. Let us begin seizing every day for this purpose.

Day 3
Putting It into Practice

It's your turn. Just as you read my journaling of yesterday, I ask you to use today to record your conversations with God throughout it and the opportunities you have to know Him in it. My day happened to be a busy one, but God makes Himself known in all of our days. I pray this exercise will be a tremendous blessing. Do remember that when trying something new, we aren't always good at it initially. As I mentioned in day 1, this is a practice we seek to develop. It's a practice God is very pleased with and one in which He will meet you. I've given you these two pages along with verses in the margin to encourage you along the way. Be blessed!

"Come near to God and He will come near to you."
James 4:8

"This is eternal life, that they know You the only true God and Jesus whom You sent." John 17:3

Day 4
Knowing the Fullness of God

*So there are three witnesses in heaven: the Father, the Word
and the Holy Spirit, and these three are One; and there are
three witnesses on the earth: the Spirit, the water, and the
blood; and these three agree. (1 John 5:7–8 AMP)*

God has chosen to reveal His fullness in the three forms of God
the Father, God the Son, and God the Holy Spirit. Our intimate
knowing of Him will be enhanced as we see and seek Him in these
three forms.

God the Father
It was what Jesus called God when He gave the disciples a model
prayer to teach them how to pray. It's interesting to me that of all the
things they could ask Jesus to teach them, prayer was what they asked.
What had they observed in how Jesus prayed that they had neither seen
nor experienced? Could it be intimacy? Was Jesus talking to His loving
Father rather than talking at or speaking about an angry, judgmental
God that needed to be pleased or appeased?

In His intimate Father and Son relationship, Jesus revered God.
The relationship was intimate, but it was not casual. Jesus said He came
to do the will of His Father: "I do nothing on My own but speak just
what the Father has taught Me" (John 8:28). He also came to give the
Father glory: "I have brought You glory on earth by completing the
work You gave Me to do" (John 17:4).

Consider God's role as your heavenly Father. God is not like our
earthly fathers, good or bad. He is God and therefore the perfect
Father. Rest in this fact, and may you gain deeper understanding as to
the role He longs to play in your life. I encourage you to read slowly
and prayerfully through these verses, asking God through His Holy
Spirit to reveal new insights to you.

For each passage, give God a title or titles where needed, with a
short description of the role:

> God The
> Father

Psalm 144:1–2

Psalm 68:5

Matthew 7:11, James 1:17

Romans 8:38–39

Proverbs 3:11–12

Psalm 16:11

Psalm 78:4

Jesus, God the Son

"Behold, the Lamb of God who takes away the sins of the world" (John 1:29). Jesus came to earth as the image of the invisible God. He is called the Word, the Word who became flesh and made His dwelling among man. He was with God in the beginning, and through Him all things were created (from John 1).

His coming was prophesied in Genesis 3:15, and in God's perfect timing, He was born of a virgin and raised by her and a carpenter. He grew in wisdom and stature and in favor with God and man, and then at an earthly age of approximately thirty years old, He began a three-year public ministry. It was the work set out for Him by God since the beginning of time.

John 1:12

John 14:6, 10:10

John 8:12

John 10:14–15

John 1:17

Philippians 4:19

2 Corinthians 5:18, Colossians 1:22

We will pick up tomorrow with the role of God, the Holy Spirit. Will you conclude today by pondering these roles of God in your own life? We'll look at these roles tomorrow.

Day 5
God's Indwelling Presence

The role of the Holy Spirit is sometimes the least understood. He is called by many names, including Spirit, Spirit of God, Spirit of Christ, Holy Ghost, and Spirit of the Lord. He is the indwelling presence of God promised by Jesus and whose coming Jesus said was better than Him remaining on earth. The Holy Spirit's coming was prophesied in the Old Testament. Before His ascension, Jesus told the disciples to go to Jerusalem and wait for the Holy Spirit, with His arrival causing quite a stir among the people. With the Holy Spirit's coming, the apostles operated under a greater power.

Like yesterday, give a title and brief description of each of the following roles.

God, the Holy Spirit

John 14:17, 16:13

John 14:16, 26

John 16:13-14

Romans 8: 26-27

2 Thessalonians 2:13

1 Corinthians 6:19

**God,
the Holy
Spirit**

Our study this week is focused on going beyond just obtaining knowledge of God and instead progressing into living, moving, and having our being in Him. Please go through the title lists you made both today and yesterday, and record both the roles and the ways you have experienced Him in those roles. Begin with how you experienced Him in your day of journaling earlier this week. I encourage you also to note the way in which you were drawn into deeper intimacy with God through your experience of Him.

Conclusion

In week 1, we looked at Paul's passion to know Christ. It was a passion he sought to live out by living as Jesus did, living and moving and having his being in God. May his words from Philippians 3:7–14 inspire us.

But whatever were gains to me I now consider loss for the sake of Christ. What is more, I consider everything a loss because of the surpassing worth of knowing Christ Jesus my Lord, for whose sake I have lost all things. I consider them garbage, that I may gain Christ and be found in Him, not having a righteousness of my own that comes from the law, but that which is through faith in Christ—the righteousness that comes from God on the basis of faith. I want to know Christ—yes, to know the power of His resurrection and participation in His sufferings, becoming like Him in His death, and so, somehow, attaining to the resurrection from the dead. Not that I have already obtained all this, or have already arrived at my goal, but I press on to take hold of that for which Christ Jesus took hold of me. Brothers and sisters, I do not consider myself yet to have taken hold of it. But one thing I do: forgetting what is behind and straining toward what is ahead, I press on toward the goal to win the prize for which God has called me heavenward in Christ Jesus.

Will you press on? We pursue many things in this life. May we seek God first, seeking to know Him as we live and move and have our being in Him, and avoid living life backward by fitting Him in last. "Seek first the kingdom of God and His righteousness. Then all these things will be added unto us" (Matt. 6:33).

Notes

Week 7
Talking With God

Day 1
A Two-Way Conversation

Picture the scene: you and I meet at a local coffeehouse. I rush in, frazzled as I think about the upcoming events of the day. My burdens are many, and I quickly, almost forcefully, pour them out on you. I barely even say hello. I never ask how you are doing.

Even still, your heart is tender toward me, for you understand what I am feeling. You've experienced similar trials. You long to share the wisdom God has given you, but I don't give you any opportunity to speak. When it appears my long discourse may be ending, you prepare to share. Yet, it's not to be; it's time for me to go, and I rush off with the same abruptness with which I arrived. You sit, dazed. "What just happened?" you wonder. Whatever it was, a conversation didn't happen.

Let me ask: Has your time with God ever resembled the scene above? Mine has. I've rushed in, even feeling a little proud that I've made time for a "quiet time" in the first place. Then I talk;

I talk and talk and talk. All the while God, who already knows all of my thoughts and my needs, is given no time to speak. No fellowship occurred because no interaction occurred. My relationship with Him and my knowledge of Him went no deeper.

Do you give God the opportunity to speak? Or perhaps it's better to ask, do you listen to what God is saying? Have you ever considered prayer to be a two-way conversation with God? I am amazed at the privilege that is given us as children of God to talk with Almighty God. Yet just as we may do with other parts of life or other people in our lives, we can take it for granted and misuse or fail to see its value and purpose. Today we will look at both the purpose and privilege of talking with God. I pray you will see this privilege in a whole new light.

The Purpose

The development of our relationship with God is like that of any relationship in which we are seeking intimacy: we spend time together so we can come to know one another. Go back to week 1 or week 6, and record the meaning of the word "know" as it is often used in Scripture:

Ponder for a few minutes the relationships in which you enjoy the greatest intimacy. Why are those relationships so close? Record your thoughts below:

As we see in John 17:3, Jesus said the experience of the life of God in us (eternal life) comes as we know the one true God and Jesus, whom He sent. Considering that God already knows everything about us, it makes sense that the focus of our conversations with Him would be for us to come to know Him better: to know His heart, His joys, His desires, His character, His will, and His ways. While all elements of prayer, including presenting our requests, are important, it's quite possible that most of us have missed the highest privilege given us through prayer: coming into an intimate knowledge through first-hand experience with Almighty God, our heavenly Father, the lover of our soul.

Not only has God shown Himself as a triune God—Father, Son, and Holy Spirit—but He also relates to us specifically in the numerous aspects of His nature. As we spend time with God, seeking to know

It makes sense that the focus of our conversations with God would be for us to come to know Him better.

Him, we come to know Him as friend, shepherd/guide, lover, provider, counselor, defender ... We see how He sees us and experience all He wants to lavish on us, simply because we show up, seek Him, and receive.

The Psalmist came to God panting for Him. Read Psalm 42:1–2, and then write a prayer to God below. Share with Him your honest thoughts and needs in response to these verses:

The Privilege
Have you considered the privilege of who wants to spend time in conversation with you? King David did. Read his words in Psalm 8:3–4, and then express your feelings regarding God's desire to spend time talking with you:

Consider also that God not only wants to spend time with you, but He also wants to be in continual communion and conversation with you. Record your insights from 1 Thessalonians 5:17:

What phrases in 1 Thessalonians 5:16–18 indicate part of what our ongoing conversation with God should include?

If you feel the need, write a prayer to God below expressing your regret for a misplaced focus of your prayers. If the coffeehouse story was an accurate picture, ask God to lead you in a new direction. Ask Him to help you listen more so you can know Him more. We'll look at the practice of this later this week.

> *As we spend time with God, we see how He sees us and we experience all He wants to lavish on us.*

Tomorrow we will look at how God spoke in the Old Testament. On day 3, we'll look at God's new (or renewed) way of talking with His people in the new covenant. May God bless you and prepare you because we will end this week seeking to either begin or continue a life-long journey of listening to God and enjoying two-way conversation with Him.

Day 2
God Spoke

In the Old Testament, God spoke largely through the prophets, though it was not His first desire. God's desire was to speak to His people personally, an intimacy seen in Genesis 3:8–9 from what Adam and Eve lost. The man and his wife heard the sound of the Lord God as He was walking in the garden in the cool of the day, and they hid from the Lord God among the trees of the garden. But the Lord God called to the man, "Where are you?"

Intimacy was lost because of sin. God, however, did not give up on mankind.

Though little is said about him, we are told, "Enoch walked with God, then he was no more, because God took him away" (Gen. 5:23). Wickedness continued to spread, causing God to grieve that He had made man—the mankind with whom He had longed for intimacy. "I will wipe mankind, whom I have created, from the face of the earth—men and animals and creatures that move along the ground, and the birds of the air—for I am grieved that I have made them. But Noah found favor in the eyes of the Lord" (Gen. 6:5-8).

God shared His plans with Noah, instructing Noah to build an ark on which to save himself, his family, and two of every living creature. As the earth repopulated following the flood, evil spread once again. God chose for Himself a people, a nation, choosing a man named Abraham as the father of this great nation. The closeness God shared with him is expressed as Abraham being called "a friend of God" (James 2:23).

The closeness God shared with Abraham is expressed as Abraham is called "a friend of God."

After more than four hundred years in slavery in Egypt, God led His people, Abraham's descendants, out of bondage and on a journey into a land He would give them—the Promised Land. It was on this journey that God desired to establish intimacy with the people of this nation. Yet they would choose otherwise. Having heard the voice of God, they were frightened of Him, wanting Moses to go between them and God. Read Deuteronomy 5:22–29. From 5:22–25, describe the Israelites' experience:

The experience frightened them. What did they request of Moses in 5:27?

This ushered in the era of God speaking largely through the prophets. Let's seek to know God and His ways as we look into the lives of three prophets and how God spoke to them.

Read the following passages. They are written to God's prophets who were called to speak to the nations. From studying them, we can learn of God's creative ways of speaking to His people and to whom He speaks. May they make us open to ways He may choose to speak to us. Record your insights from each passage.

Samuel
Read 1 Samuel 3.

Jeremiah
Read Jeremiah 18:1–6.

Isaiah

Read Isaiah 6:1–8. What was the state of Isaiah's heart when God spoke?

> "No longer will a man teach his neighbor, or a man his brother, saying, 'Know the LORD,' because they will all know Me, from the least of them to the greatest," declares the LORD. "For I will forgive their wickedness and will remember their sins no more."
> Jeremiah 31:34

Though God spoke through the prophets for a time, He never resigned Himself from sharing such intimacy with all people. God's interaction and relationship with each person are unique, which is a precious aspect of our God. Through this quick look at how God spoke to the prophets, we gain insight into the creative ways He may choose to speak to us. As children of God under the new covenant, this special privilege is now available to us.

Read Jeremiah 31:33–34. Meditate on it by prayerfully rereading it several times. Then ask God to speak to you about what this Scripture means for you:

Day 3
God Still Speaks

Jesus spent much of His last three years on earth walking and talking with His disciples. They often traveled on foot, up to thirty, fifty, or even seventy miles at a time. Imagine the conversations that invariably took place. I've often wished I could walk and talk with Jesus as the disciples did—to see, touch, and hear Him in a physical sense. Yet Jesus said what you and I have available to us is better: "I tell you the truth: It is for your good that I am going away. Unless I go away the Counselor will not come to you, but if I do I will send Him to you" (John 16:7).

Jesus' words recorded in John 16:5–16 show how the work Jesus began (16:8–11, conviction of sin) and the fellowship the disciples shared with Him would continue and be available to us today. Read

John 16:5–16, and record from verses 12–16 what we have today through the Counselor/Holy Spirit:

This role is not new to the Holy Spirit. Record your findings from 2 Peter 1:20–21:

Today's lesson is by no means exhaustive on how God speaks. My desire is to give you enough information and a model of its practice to lead you into your own journey of intimacy with God through hearing His voice. I encourage you to begin chronicling how God speaks to you. This one practice has profound implications for understanding God's desire to be intimate with us.

God speaks through His Word as the Holy Spirit reveals truth to our hearts. This is what Jesus was speaking about in John 16:5–16. As we submit ourselves to reading, studying, meditating on, and hearing God's Word, the Holy Spirit will take the inspired Word of God and speak it to us as a specific word. This is a word specifically for us at a specific time and/or specific situation. I have experienced this as certain passages will grab my heart as I read them, taking on an enhanced and/or specific meaning for application.

As we "hide God's Word in our hearts that we might not sin against Him" (Ps. 119:11), the Holy Spirit can also bring it to our mind for specific application and/or wisdom, even when we are not reading the Word of God at that moment.

God speaks through promptings as the Holy Spirit moves in our hearts. One of the first times I remember this happening was many years ago. While traveling back from my parents' house in Alabama where I had spent spring break with our three children, I sensed God saying, "Pray for the safety of all driving back for the Bible study this evening." So I prayed. At the time I began praying, I was alongside

> *God speaks as I quiet my heart, ask Him to speak, and then listen.*

> *God speaks through His Word as the Holy Spirit reveals truth to our heart.*

> *God speaks through promptings as the Holy Spirit moves in our heart.*

another van on the interstate. As I prayed, I moved about twenty-five yards ahead. As I finished praying, the van I had just been next to had a back tire blow out and they fishtailed into the exact place I had just been. Coincidence? I don't think so. God, through His Spirit, prompted me to pray. Since we were going sixty-five mph, I feel confident He saved all of our lives.

God speaks as I quiet my heart, ask Him to speak, and then listen. God did this with Elijah in 1 Kings 19:9–18. As conditions around him included an earthquake and fire, Elijah pulled his cloak over his face, and in listening, he heard God speak. It is this method of hearing that we will study and seek tomorrow.

God is the same yesterday, today, and forever (Heb. 13:8). Where He once spoke to His people, He still speaks. Take a few minutes to review, and ask God to speak to you about all you have studied so far this week. Record what God shows you below:

Day 4
Be Still and Know I Am God

These words from Psalm 46:10 are also apt instructions as we seek to listen and hear the voice of God for our purpose of knowing Him. Begin your study today by reading all of Psalm 46. How did God speak to you through these verses?

Dear friend, what I am about to share with you is one of the sweetest gifts God has ever given me. Please take today's lesson as a basic outline of how to come into the presence of God and open yourself up to hear His voice. Let God tailor it for you, and be willing to laugh at yourself if you feel awkward. I seem to be awkward whenever I try something new, and the ease with which I now enjoy this has come over time. Just stick with it.

Like Samuel, let us come, excited to say, "Speak Lord, Your servant is listening." There is no one exclusive way to listen to God, for God is personal to each one of us. I have found, however, the following method to be helpful to me and others I know. I encourage you to read through the process first and then come back and seek to put it into practice. As you do, ask God to lead you by His Spirit. He has a special time planned for you! Space is provided for you to record your prayer if you desire.

Enter His presence with reverence through thanksgiving and praise. Psalm 8 would be a wonderful psalm to begin with.

You come as a priest. Present yourself cleansed. Praying Psalm 51 is a beautiful way to seek a clean, pure heart before God. Be open to any sin He may bring to your mind, and confess it.

As long as you desire to or feel it's necessary, I encourage you to spend time worshipping God through the above two acts. When your spirit feels settled and ready, profess your belief to God that He is a God who speaks with man.

In Hebrews 12:18–25a, the author speaks of the time in history we studied (Deut. 5:22–29), during which the Israelites rejected hearing God speak. He challenges those under the new covenant to know that we come at a new time. May God give you great understanding to grasp the fullness of these words:

"You have not come to a mountain that can be touched and that is burning with fire … or to such a voice speaking words that those who heard it begged that no further word be spoken to them … But you have come to Mount Zion, to the heavenly Jerusalem, the city of the living God. You have come to thousands upon thousands of angels in joyful assembly, to the church of the firstborn, whose names are written in heaven. You have come to God, the judge of all men, to the spirits of righteous men made perfect, to Jesus the mediator

"Speak Lord, Your servant is listening."
1 Samuel 3:10

of a new covenant, and to the sprinkled blood that speaks a better word than the blood of Abel. See to it that you do not refuse Him who speaks."

Come now with confidence, professing your belief that God desires to and will speak with you, asking Him also to silence all voices but His own.

As you come to God, still and with anticipation, be aware of spontaneous thoughts that come upon your mind. I encourage you to write them in the space below just as they flow from your mind. Do not stop to analyze them. Do not worry whether or not they make sense. Simply write. You can go back and read them later. (It will be very helpful to do this in a quiet place.)

As you consider the words you have written, remember that God wants to speak to you. As your trust and confidence in Him grow, you will hear more. Also remember that God never contradicts His Word. If anything written is not consistent with Scripture, you can be confident it did not come from God. Simply disregard it.

As precious as it is to hear God's voice, I encourage you also to learn to be content simply sitting in His presence. I often come to God, having walked through the steps of praise and confession, and lay my thoughts and even my needs before Him, and then I sit, content to be in His presence. If He wants to speak—great. If He wants to speak to one of my concerns—that's great too. Yet if He simply wants me to be with Him or He wants to say something unrelated to my sharing—that is great as well! He is God, and I want to hear what He wants to say, especially if that something is, "I love you; just be with Me."

What thoughts and emotions are you having following this exercise? Write them and tell God:

As seen in the coffee shop story in day 1, intimacy develops through two-way conversation as we spend time—both quality and a good quantity of time—with God. A close relationship with God takes time, as does your ability to listen and discern the voice of God. Be patient with yourself, and keep coming back, day after day, to sit with and hear from God.

Day 5
Speak, Lord

Your work for today, like yesterday, is to be with and seek to hear the voice of God. I've written the basic outline to guide you. If God is adding to it or changing it in some manner for you, I encourage you to make note of those changes on the following pages.

As you come to Him, consider beginning with a short time of worshipping God with music. Then visualize yourself coming into His presence. You may see Him as Isaiah did (Isa. 6:1–4), high and exalted on His throne, with the train of His robe filling the temple—yet you are invited to come close. You may see Him along the Sea of Galilee as recorded in Matthew 4:18–20, coming to talk to you as He did for the first time with Peter and Andrew. You may even see Him as the children did in Luke 18:15, with Jesus saying, "Let the little children [her] come to Me and do not hinder them [her], for the kingdom of God belongs to ones such as these [her]."

There is space provided for you to write your prayer at each step; do what is most natural to you. However, recording the spontaneous thoughts that come upon your mind is important, both for remembrance and to later check to ensure what you heard is consistent with God's Word and therefore was His voice speaking.

Enter His presence with reverence through thanksgiving and praise.

Come as a priest; present yourself cleansed.

When your spirit feels settled and ready, profess your belief to God that He is a God who speaks with man. Come with confidence, professing your belief that God desires to and will speak with you, asking Him also to silence all voices but His own. Record the spontaneous thoughts that come to your mind.

God's written Word in the Holy Scriptures should always take preeminence when knowing God and being guided in His will and His ways. How God speaks is not what is important; that God speaks with us is what is important. God speaks through nature, through His written Word, and also through others. Be open to hearing God's voice in His multitude of ways throughout every day.

Conclusion

Now this is eternal life: that they may know You, the only true God and Jesus Christ, whom You sent. (John 17:3)

Consider the word may in this verse. We may know Him. We are invited to know Him; it's our choice. In pondering this verse, I think of another verse (Rev. 3:20) in which Jesus says: "Here I am! I stand at the door and knock. If anyone opens the door I will come in and eat with him, and he with Me."

Let's go back and reset the scene that opened this lesson—the coffeehouse conversation. This time picture yourself having coffee with God and the monologue is now a dialogue. Your focus has shifted. You want to know more about Him; you want to know what He has to say to you. Imagine for a moment what He might say. Anticipate getting to know how He feels about you.

In Jesus' prayer recorded in John 17, He says: "I have made You known to them and will continue to make You known in order that the love You have for Me may be in them and that I myself may be in them" (John 17:26).

By increasingly knowing God, you will grow in knowing the fullness of His love and the fullness of Christ living in you.

Notes

Week 8
Our Royal Identity

Day 1
Children of God

My husband and I have three children, and because they are our children, they have certain rights and privileges. Until each reached the age of eighteen, by law they had rights for their basic needs of food, shelter, and clothing to be overseen by us. They had the right under our care to be free from physical, mental, and emotional abuse, as well as the right to a state-funded education and some form of health care. They had legal rights, and we had legal responsibilities. They've also been given certain privileges. There are things we do for them and give them and a relationship we share with them that we do not share with others, simply because they are our children.

The same is true for us as children of God. John 1:12 says, "Yet to all who received Him [Jesus], to those who believed in His name, He gave the right to become children of God." As 1 John 3:1 says, "And that is what we are!" As a child of God, you enjoy specific rights and privileges with God that others have forfeited by not choosing Him as their Lord and Savior.

Our focus this week is on our royal identity. We will look briefly at our identity in Christ: an identity established because we are children of God. It is our new DNA as "children born not of natural descent, nor of human decision or a husband's will, but born of God" (John 1:13). Then we will consider a special privilege we have been given as children of God and the power of God available to and in us. It is through our belief in this identity and living by our true identity that our intimacy with God greatly increases. So let's get started.

In Ephesians 2, Paul gives a wonderful comparison of our life before Christ and our life now in Christ. In the space below, record what you find:

Ephesians 2

Before Christ I was:

In Christ I am

For extra study: Add to your list above of "In Christ I am" from Ephesians 1:3–14.

Please end your time today praising God for your new DNA. I encourage you to select a few specific things and tell God how and why you are grateful for them.

"How great is the love the Father has lavished on us, that we should be called children of God! And that is what we are! The reason the world does not know us is that it did not know Him."
1 John 3:1

Day 2
Heirs of the Promise

We sat with a group of women broken from bad choices and difficult circumstances. We begged them to remember that the sum of their choices does not determine who they are. While their choices brought them to a recovery home for women, their choices did not change who they are. For you see, these women are followers of Jesus and therefore daughters of God, heirs of God's promise with a royal identity.

Read Galatians 3:26–29, and record your insights below:

God's promise to Abraham was that He would make him into a great nation, and through him, all people on the earth would be blessed (Gen. 12:1–3). With this promise, God was speaking of the coming of Jesus, the Messiah through whom God would fulfill His promises to Abraham. Scripture repeatedly says, "Abraham believed God and it was credited to him as him as righteousness." (Rom 4:3) Our righteousness, like Abraham's, comes by faith in Jesus Christ.

Read Romans 3:21–22, and record your insights below:

This was the mystery revealed to Paul. It was the message which he was called to preach to the Gentiles. "This mystery is that through the gospel the Gentiles are heirs together with Israel, members together of one body, and sharers together in the promise in Christ Jesus" (Eph. 3:6). "The mystery that has been kept hidden for generations, but is now disclosed to the saints … To them God has chosen to make known among the Gentiles the glorious riches of this mystery which is Christ in you, the hope of glory" (Col. 1:26–27).

Our "goodness" is not the issue. Our good or bad choices don't include or exclude us in God's family. Our faith in Jesus does, and His righteousness imparted to us makes us heirs of God's promise. Read Ephesians 2:8–9, and record your insights below:

"This righteousness from God comes through faith in Jesus Christ to all who believe." Romans 3:22

96

We are sons and daughters of God because of our faith in Jesus. An ever-increasing awareness of our identity in Christ is essential to our journey of intimacy with God. As heirs, we are now part of that great nation—a nation in God's present kingdom on this earth through which He desires, through intimate relationships, to give back to His children the dominion forfeited by Adam and Eve in the garden of Eden.

It's the relationship God originally designed man to have with Him. God has always wanted men and women He could depend on to be His vessels to bring His will to earth. As we walk in our true identity as co-laborers with God, we will find our intimacy with God increasing. Just as it is in earthly relationships, time spent together and priorities aligned will draw us closer together.

The truths presented today are foundational. If our righteousness depended on us, most of us would never consider coming into God's presence, much less approaching His throne of grace with confidence, as you will be challenged to do tomorrow.

Conclude today's lesson by sharing your thoughts with God about being His child, an heir of His promise.

Day 3
The Throne of Grace

In day 1's listing of "In Christ I am," you may have noted from Ephesians 2:18–19 that you are now a member of God's household, and as a result, you have access to God. Hebrews 4:16 describes this special access: "Let us then approach the throne of grace with confidence so that we may receive mercy and find grace to help us in our time of need."

This invitation to approach the throne of grace is based on our royal identity. Once dead in our sins, objects of wrath, and separated from God, we are now alive in Christ, reconciled to God, and brought near to Him through the blood of Jesus.

I recall an occasion on which one of our children came home from a friend's house very upset from events that happened there. She'd hidden her emotions until walking in our front door, where a flood of tears let loose. In thinking back and considering that scene in light of the verse above, she'd come home—to a place where she hoped to find mercy. She was looking for grace to help her in her time of need.

Mercy comes from the Greek word *eleos* and means kindness or goodwill toward the miserable and the afflicted, joined with a desire to help them.[1] Grace comes from the Greek word *charis* and means merciful kindness by which God, exerting His holy influence, turns us to Christ and keeps and strengthens us.[2] Another definition is unmerited divine assistance or favor. The throne of grace spoken of in Hebrews 4:16 represents a literal throne seat on which Christ sits.

Combine these definitions, and summarize what you are invited to approach and what you can expect to find there:

Now read Hebrews 4:14–16 and Romans 8:26–28. Expanding on what you wrote above, write an explanation of the privilege you have as a child of God, one you could share with another person.

This Hebrews 4 text is part of a larger text about entering into God's rest. Rest is *katapausis* in the Greek, and it means a resting place. It is described as a heavenly blessedness in which God dwells and that He has promised to make persevering Christians partakers of.[3] I believe we can also define rest as an aspect of God's grace. We cease from our flesh-driven striving and receive His unmerited favor and power to do the work through us.

Read Hebrews 3 and 4 and then answer the questions. According to Hebrews 3:1, to whom is the writer speaking?

Summarize the warning in Hebrews 3:7–11:

In Hebrews 3:12–19, the question is asked, "And to whom did God swear that they would never enter His rest?" (v.18). What two words in these verses describe these people?

What one-summary word is given in 3:19?

In what aspect of your life do you need to approach the throne of grace?

Is there unbelief keeping you from doing it? If there is, I encourage you to let the Word of God reveal to you the truth. Hebrews 4:12 tells us, "The word of God is living and active. Sharper than any double-edged sword, it penetrates even to dividing soul and spirit, joints and marrow; it judges the thoughts and attitudes of the heart." Let God's Word cut through any unbelief you may be having. If you needed this step, write your area of unbelief below, and then record the truth from God's Word.

Approach God on His throne of grace with confidence. Before you pick up your phone to talk to a friend, run to God. Go even as a child running through her own front door, finally able to release her tears and fears, so He can give you His very best. He will reach down and wipe your tears; in His strength, He will carry you and get you to the place where you can walk again on solid ground.

Allow yourself to be blessed as you receive mercy and find grace to help in your time of need.

Day 4
God's Unlimited Supply

One day while pondering God's words in Hebrews 4:16, "Let us approach the throne of grace with confidence so that we may receive mercy and find grace to help us in our time of need," a picture came to my mind. I saw myself walking up to God, and behind Him was a massive storehouse. It looked like warehouses I see today, but it was many miles long. As I looked at this storehouse, I sensed God saying, "Come and ask; My supply is unlimited." It was a scene I later found described in Deuteronomy 28:12: "The Lord will open the houses, the storehouses of His bounty."

As I continued to ponder this scene, Matthew 7:7–12 came to my mind.

Ask and it will be given to you; seek and you will find; knock and the door will be opened to you. For everyone who asks receives; the one who seeks finds; and to the one who knocks, the door will be opened. Which of you, if your son asks for bread, will give him a stone? Or if he asks for a fish, will give him a snake? If you, then, though you are evil, know how to give good gifts to your children, how much more will your Father in heaven give good gifts to those who ask Him! So in everything, do to others what you would have them do to you, for this sums up the Law and the Prophets.

Simply because our children are our children, my husband and I desire to give them good things. In fact, we've never intentionally withheld something we felt would be good for them. However, they've certainly not been given everything they've ever asked for because in some cases, we determined it wasn't best for them. It wasn't a "good gift." God does the same with us as our heavenly Father.

"Come and ask; my supply is unlimited."

In the context of this passage, it is clear that one reason the good gifts (the bounty as I saw it in God's enormous storehouse) aren't given to us is because we haven't asked, we haven't sought, and we haven't knocked. In fact, the Greek meaning of the words ask, seek, and knock is best explained in the Amplified Version: "Ask and keep on asking; seek and keep on seeking; knock and keep on knocking." In other words, we haven't approached the throne of grace consistently and been persistent there to find the mercy and grace—the kindness and unmerited divine assistance and supply we need.

Yet as children of God, those with a royal identity, not only is this something we can do, but it's something we should do. Stop to consider: Has not God, at least in part, chosen to meet our needs in response to our prayers? This is so that "we would seek Him and perhaps reach out for Him and find Him, though He is not far from each one of us. For in Him [so that in Him] we live and move and have our being. As some of your own poets have said, we are His offspring" (Acts 17:27–28). Has He not done so in order to have intimacy with us?

What are you asking God for right now? Have you grown weary from asking? Have you stopped seeking? Are you no longer knocking? What is it you should be taking to the throne of grace? If specific thoughts are coming to your mind, record them below. Give them to God, and give Him the opportunity to pour out His abundance to you.

> *Ask*
> *Seek*
> *Knock*

Matthew 7:12, written in the context of asking, seeking, and knocking, is also an excellent reminder that we are to approach God's throne of grace not only for ourselves but also for others: "So in everything, do to others as you would have them do to you, for this sums up the Law and the Prophets."

John 2:1–11 gives the account of Mary, the mother of Jesus, going directly to Jesus (the throne of grace on earth then) to find help in a time of need. Read this passage, and answer the questions below:

Why did Mary approach Jesus?

How did Mary approach Jesus?

> *John 2:1-11*

What was unusual about Jesus' response to Mary?

What was unusual about the miracle (other than it being miraculous)?

How would you describe the miracle?

What was a result of this miraculous provision that came in response to Mary's request?

What can you learn from this event about approaching the throne of grace with confidence?

> *"Now to Him Who is able to do immeasurably more than we ask or imagine according to His power that is at work within us."*
> *Ephesians 3:20*

Day 5
God's Incomparably Great Power

In his letter to the church at Ephesus, Paul, in praying for the people, describes God's power. He calls it an incomparably great power that is like the working of God's mighty strength, which He exerted in Christ when He raised Him from dead and seated Him at His right hand in the heavenly realms. It's a power that placed Jesus far above all rule and authority, power and dominion, and placed all things under Jesus' feet, and appointed Him to be over everything (Eph. 1:19–22).

That power is manifested in us who believe! Notice the phrase "exerted in Christ." As you journey in intimacy with God, will you allow Him to exert this power in you?

God's Power over Sin

A vital part of your royal identity is that as a child of God, the power of sin over you has been broken. Read Romans 6, and record below and in the margin everything written concerning your relationship to sin. As you work through this exercise, ask God to reveal these deep truths not only to your mind but to your heart.

His Power Exerted Through Us

Ephesians 3:20 says, "[God] is able to do immeasurably more than we ask or imagine, according to His power that is at work within us."

Record the working of God's power within men in the following passages. Be inspired!

Acts 4:33

Acts 6:8

1 Corinthians 2:5

2 Corinthians 13:4

Conclusion

Understanding our royal identity plays a huge part in how we relate to God and therefore the intimacy we experience with Him. As we come to His throne of grace, we will begin walking in greater dependence upon Him. Just as independence from God is a primary barrier to intimacy, coming to God's throne of grace and depending on Him to meet your needs is a primary part of your journey in intimacy with Him.

Along with an ongoing chorus of praise and thanksgiving and talking with God, let coming to God's throne of grace become a daily part of your journey. You may be confident of this promise in Philippians 4:19:

"And my God will meet all your needs according to His riches in Christ Jesus."

Notes

Week 9
The Vine and the Branch

Day 1
God Wants a Vineyard

We can learn a lot from the Old Testament about God's plans for the world as He first sought to fulfill them through the nation of Israel. As we turn our focus this week to the biblical illustration of Jesus as the vine and us as branches (John 15), we're going to begin by considering God's desire for a people who would be like a vineyard to Him.

God looked first to Israel. Read Isaiah 5:1–7. As verse 7 states, "The vineyard of the Lord is the house of Israel, and the men of Judah are the garden of His delight." At this time in history, the nation of Israel was divided into two nations: the Northern Kingdom (Israel, ten tribes) and the Southern Kingdom (Judah, two tribes). The wording used makes the vineyard description inclusive of both. Yet as the verse goes on to say, "And He looked for justice, but saw bloodshed; for righteousness, but heard cries of distress." Much of what Scripture records is Israel's failure to be the vineyard God desired. That is the case in the Isaiah 5 passage as God asks Israel to consider whether He was the cause of their bad fruit or if they were. His question is rhetorical because He had just stated His affection for His vineyard and His care of it. God wanted them to understand their responsibility for their condition.

Now God looks to all who, through faith like Abraham, believe in and receive Jesus and thereby become heirs of the promise of Abraham. Last week we studied God's promise to Abraham that through him, God would build a great nation and all nations on the earth would be blessed (Gen. 12:1–3). Jesus is the promised one through whom this great nation would be fulfilled, and is described or prophesied in Isaiah 11:1 as "a shoot [which] will come up from the stump of Jesse [father of David and therefore from the line of David]; from his roots a Branch will bear fruit."

Read Isaiah 11:1–11. In this passage, God is speaking both about Jesus, the coming Messiah, and the kingdom He will one day establish and rule over. From 11:2–3, list below characteristics of His reign because, as it begins in verse 2: "The Spirit of the Lord will rest on him …"

> *As a branch of the one true vine, God wants to bear fruit through you.*

Though we can never compare ourselves to Jesus, in our royal identity, such characteristics can be true about us. As heirs of the promise of Abraham, what God desired through the nation of Israel, He now also desires to do through His people today. As a branch of the one true vine, God wants to bear fruit through you, including the fruit of wisdom, understanding, counsel, power, knowledge, and fear of the Lord—even a delight in the fear of the Lord. The Isaiah 11 passage speaks also of righteousness being Jesus' belt and faithfulness the sash around His waist (v. 5). God desires to produce all of these, as well as the fruit of the Spirit spoken of in Galatians 5:22–23, in His heirs.

Imagine for a moment that there is a variety of fruit in your life that others can pick and be nourished from—those whom God has placed in your life, around whom you live and move and have your being in the specific time and place God has placed you. What a privilege it would be for others to pick from your life such fruit as wisdom regarding a specific situation they are going through; understanding of God's Word; godly counsel; power to do what God is calling them to do; and a deeper knowledge of God. Imagine them seeing a display of how delightful it is to fear God (be in awe of, trust, obey, and worship Him). This is possible because the Branch from Jesse is in you. It occurs as you yield to His life (described as the true vine in John 15:1 and 5), and it flows through you, the branch (John 15:5).

Tomorrow we are going to consider what it looks like to live as a branch. Yet before doing so, conclude your time today with a look at God's care for those who are willing to stay connected to Jesus and become a thriving part of His vineyard. Record your findings from Isaiah 27:2–3 and Isaiah 5:1–7, considering also what care Israel lost (5:5–6).

Take a few minutes to consider the intimacy you will experience with God as you allow Him to care for you as the above passages illustrate, as you experience (know) His life flowing through you, and as you see the evidence of this in your life as you bear fruit. Remember that this is fruit others can pick and be nourished from. Let God begin to form a vision for you in your life as a branch. Record your thoughts below:

Day 2
Life as a Branch

I am the true vine and my Father is the gardener. He cuts off every branch in Me that bears no fruit, while every branch that does bear fruit He prunes so that it can be even more fruitful. You are already clean because of the word I have spoken to you. Remain in Me, and I will remain in you. No branch can bear fruit by itself; it must remain

I am the vine; you are the branches. If a man remains in Me and I in him, he will bear much fruit; apart from Me you can do nothing."
John 15:5

in the vine. Neither can you bear fruit unless you remain in Me. I am the vine; you are the branches. If a man remains in Me and I in him, he will bear much fruit; apart from Me you can do nothing. (John 15:1–5)

Called the Branch of Jesse in Isaiah 11, Jesus is now called the Vine in John 15. He who came to show and teach us about oneness with the Father uses an illustration from nature to teach us how. As we first come into a better understanding of Jesus as the vine and then begin to know Jesus as our vine through first-hand experience, deeper intimacy will follow.

In as literal a sense as possible, I want you to consider your life as compared to a branch on the vine or tree. To begin, record your observations about a branch below. Any tree branch in your yard will do.

Allow me to share a few of my observations. A branch comes out of the tree trunk. Leaves come out of it, birds sit on it, and squirrels climb on it. It looks prettier with leaves. The branch gives the tree its shape, and no two branches look exactly the same. The branches from which the sprouts have been trimmed are healthier. It couldn't exist apart from the tree. My branch has yellow leaves because of drought conditions.

Now record your observations from what Jesus says about branches in John 15:1–6:

Comparing your observations of a branch to the words of Jesus concerning you as a branch, what have you learned about yourself?

Let's expand on your description by looking at a key word in the John 15 passage: remain (NIV), abide (NASB and NKJV), and dwell/live (AMP). It's a verb from the Greek word meno, and it's used to describe a place, a state of being, or a timeframe. In the context of John 15 and Jesus' command to abide in Him, meno means to be in Him and be one with Him continually.[1]

Galatians 2:20 expands the definition even further: "I have been crucified with Christ and I no longer live, but Christ lives in me." Consider a tree branch. Does it have life in itself? Does not the life come from the tree or vine? Without the tree or vine, would it have any life? To close today's study, I want you to ponder a statement I made in day 2: "Jesus is now called the vine in John 15. He who came to show and teach us about oneness with the Father uses an illustration from nature to teach us how." As we first come into a better understanding of Jesus as the vine and then begin to know Jesus as our vine through first-hand experience, deeper intimacy will follow.

Our challenge is to better understand our role as a branch, and then, most importantly, to begin to experience our role as a branch. Doing so will enable us to experience the oneness Jesus taught, showed, and also prayed we would have. Ponder the words of Jesus below, and then talk to God about your role as a branch. Ask Him to lead you into an experiential knowledge. Then be ready for Him to do it!

> *My prayer is not for them alone [meaning His disciples]. I pray*
> *also for those who will believe in Me through their message,*
> *that they may be one, Father, just as You are in Me and I am*
> *in You. May they be in us also … that they may be one as*
> *we are one; I in them and You in me. (John 17:20–23)*

> *The vine needs the branch to bear fruit. God has chosen to need you.*

Day 3
The Purpose of the Branch

〰️

When we talk about dying and no longer living but Christ living in us, it's possible to think we have no purpose or role. Yet that is far from the truth! When I observed the tree in my yard, I noticed that the branches were what gave the tree its shape, and they were the avenue though which the tree could bear leaves and fruit. In other words, the tree/vine needs the branch to bear fruit. God has chosen to need you!

Read John 15:1–8 again, looking this time specifically for your purpose as a branch and the possibilities in that purpose. Note also God's role as gardener. Record your findings:

State specifically how God has chosen to need you.

Can you think of an example of how He has already done that through you? If so, write about it below:

I also noticed that no two branches were the same. Each is indeed quite unique. Reread two passages we have already studied, Psalm 139:13–16 and Acts 17:26–28, and relate them to your role as a branch. Record your findings below:

> You were created to produce specific fruits at a specific time in history to bless and spiritually nourish specific people.

You, as a branch and bearer of fruit, are fearfully and wonderfully made. Because you are unique, your fruit is unique. You were created to produce specific fruits at a specific time in history to bless and spiritually nourish specific people. All this was planned in advance. According to Psalm 139:16, all your days were ordained for you before one of them came into being. The Psalm continues in verse 17 to tell you God thinks about the fruit you will produce, and I bet He thinks about the effects it will have in the lives of the people He has ordained to receive it. I am also sure He imagines the pleasure and fulfillment it will bring you.

Much intimacy will come with God as He, through your role as a branch, reveals your unique design and purposes. From spiritual gifts and talents to personality types and life experiences, revel in the knowledge of God's special plans to use your fruit to increase His intimacy with you (as His life flows through you) and to bring glory to Himself: "This is to my Father's glory, that you bear much fruit, showing yourselves to be my disciples" (John 17:8).

To close today, I'd like you to dream with God a little. Ask Him to begin showing you how your unique design may be used to produce unique fruit.

Day 4
The Authority of the Branch

If you remain in Me and My words remain in you, ask whatever you wish and it will be given to you. (John 17:7)

This is some proposition! You get to ask whatever you wish and get it? The answer is yes, but two conditions precede it. What are they?

To remain in Him means I no longer live, but Christ lives in me and His words live in me (Gal. 2:20). Toward that end, Romans 12:1 explains how we enter into abiding:

Therefore, I urge you, brothers and sisters, in view of God's mercy to offer your bodies as living sacrifices, holy and pleasing to God—this is your spiritual act of worship.

We enter into abiding on a daily basis by offering our bodies as living sacrifices. Consider the words offer, living, and sacrifice separately, using a dictionary if you wish. Then put them back together and write an explanation below of what you are doing when you offer your body to God as a living sacrifice.

The Greek word for sacrifice is thysia. It is used in Romans 12:1 as a comparison between two sacrifices, such as the giving up of something you love for something you love more. When we offer our bodies as living sacrifices, we are telling God we love Him, or at least desire to love Him, more than we love ourselves. Consider this verse that describes Jesus: "Greater love has no man than this, that he lay down his life for his friends" (John 15:13). Jesus loved us more than He loved Himself. Laying down our lives as a living sacrifice to God is evidence of our love for Him.

> Laying down our life as a living sacrifice to God is evidence of our love for Him.

With our will and ways sacrificed for God's perfect will and perfect ways, His thoughts start becoming our thoughts; His desires start becoming our desires. This is what David meant when he said, "Delight yourself in the LORD and He will give you the desires of your heart" (Ps. 37:4). This is further explained in Romans 12:2: "Do not be conformed any longer to the pattern of this world, but be transformed by the renewing of your mind. Then you will be able to test and approve what God's will is—His good, pleasing and perfect will."

When we come to God in prayer as living sacrifices, we, having our minds and wills now transformed, ask for what He desires and has determined to do. We are entering into oneness, the deepest form of intimacy.

First John 5:13–15 explains this. This passage also contains several words we have examined in prior weeks. From knowledge you've gained in prior weeks, expound on the type of person who gets what he or she asks for from God. The word "believe" and phrases "eternal life" and "approaching with confidence" are key.

One way Christ's words can remain in us is through consistent time reading and studying God's Word and then meditating on it throughout the day. In doing so, we can develop a discipline of offering our minds and the thoughts that run through them as a living sacrifice. Consider how this can be done from the following two passages:

2 Corinthians 10:5

Philippians 4:8

Get Practical

To help formulate what you've been studying, write out a description of what a day could look like so you remain in Christ and His words remain in you.

Having gained a deeper understanding of what it means and looks like to remain in Christ and have His words remain in you, ask God to empower you to live in such a manner today and every day.

Day 5
The Joy of Intimacy

I have told you this so that My joy may be in you and
that your joy may be complete. (John 15:11)

We finally get back to the topic of joy!

Jesus is talking about His joy—a joy that is complete and lacking nothing because He is complete, lacking nothing. As a result of His joy being in us, we can have full joy.

What was the joy that Jesus had and longs to share with us today? I ask you to consider: is it not a joy that comes as we heed His invitation to remain as a branch, just as He did when He came to earth as the Branch of Jesse to be our sacrifice? Is it not a joy that comes in living a life—as Jesus did—that brings God glory by completing the work He gives us to do (John 17:4)? Is it not a joy obtained not from the pleasures of this world or the absence of trials and heartaches, but through becoming a living sacrifice, holy and pleasing to God and thereby living in His presence? "For there is joy in His presence, eternal pleasures at His right hand" (Ps. 16:11).

How do we finally and fully surrender to such a life and obtain the joy of Jesus? This question is answered through the context in which John 15:11 is written. Read John 15:9–17.

As the Father has loved Me, so have I loved you. Now remain in My love.
If you keep my commands, you will remain in My love, just as I have kept
My Father's commands and remain in His love. I have told you this so that
My joy may be in you and that your joy may be complete. My command
is this: Love each other as I have loved you. Greater love has no one than
this: to lay down one's life for one's friends. You are my friends if you do
what I command. I no longer call you servants, because a servant does
not know his master's business. Instead, I have called you friends, for
everything that I learned from My Father I have made known to you. You
did not choose Me, but I chose you and appointed you so that you might

*go and bear fruit—fruit that will last—and so that whatever you ask in My name the Father will give you. This is My command: **Love each other.***

In the context of John 15, the joy Jesus offers is surrounded by His command to love. John 17:26 tells us it begins by getting to know him:

> *I have made You known to them and will continue to*
> *make You known in order that the love You have for Me*
> *may be in them and I Myself may be in them.*

The journey in intimacy is a journey to know Him. The result of knowing Him is a love for Him. The result of loving Jesus is being filled with His joy as we live as the branches He created us to be.

Take a few minutes to talk to God about your desire for more joy. Share any new revelation you may have as to how you obtain joy.

Conclusion

In John 15:3, Jesus told His disciples they were already clean because of the Word He had spoken to them. They were clean, plucked from the kingdom of darkness and rescued from sin's power over them. They were placed in the kingdom of light and made righteous—all because they believed and received Him as God's Son, the long-awaited Messiah who would take away the sins of the world. If you are a follower of Jesus, you have also been plucked from the kingdom of darkness and grafted into the vine. You are a branch. Now remain, abide, dwell; live in Christ, and let Christ live in you. Be one with Him, just as He and the Father are one. Be the branch you were meant to be, and bear fruit for the world to see.

Being a branch is a role of pure dependence and requires ongoing communion with God and complete obedience to Him. There's not a better recipe for intimacy!

You have made known to me the path of life. You fill me with joy in Your presence, eternal pleasures at Your right hand. (Ps. 16:11)

"...so that My joy may be in you and that your joy may be complete." John 15:11

Notes

Week 10
Fruit Born from Abiding

Day 1
Jesus, Your Vine

When looking at great works of art, especially paintings, I often long for the ability to create something so beautiful myself—a visible expression I could share with others. The reality is such talent is not in me; in fact, even my drawings of stick people aren't very good. Yet what if the creative ability of Rembrandt or Monet were to suddenly be in me or you? Though we'd need to practice and possibly undergo training, the possibilities of creative work we could produce would be amazing. At least for me, those possibilities are far beyond those that exist now.

Such is the possibility of amazing and abundant fruit being produced from your life and mine because the life of Christ is in us. Last week we studied Jesus' illustration from nature of the vine and the branch in John 15; as a branch, we are designed to produce fruit. Yet Jesus, the vine, is the only means by which we can produce fruit that will last (John 15:16). It's fruit that's produced as the life of Christ flows through us—fruit birthed out of a position of abiding, not self-initiated striving. As Jesus increases and we decrease, more of His life, the Spirit, is released to flow through us, and oh, the fruit that His life through us will produce, beyond even the beauty of a Rembrandt or Monet painting!

For today's study, go back through last week's lesson. Summarize below what God has taught you so far about your life as a branch and His desire for you to abide. Please know that what He has been teaching you is unique to you because you are special and unique to Him. Cherish this fact as you record your insights.

> *"I am the vine; you are the branches. If a man remains in Me and I in him, he will bear much fruit."*
> *John 15:5*

Day Two
The Importance of Abiding

You were created to bear fruit—fruit that will last. God has chosen to need and use you to bear His fruit. It's for your own spiritual nourishment and blessing, as well as for those God has ordained to live and move and have their being around you. Yet without the life of the vine flowing through you, it will not happen. Summarize this truth as Jesus taught it in John 15:5–6:

Why is this true? Use the following passages to help answer this question.

Record your findings from Jeremiah 17:9:

From Galatians 5:19–21, list the fruit that the flesh produces:

Neither passage is very encouraging, but now consider each in its context. Read Jeremiah 17:5–10. How does God describe the man who lives by the flesh, by his sin nature (vv. 5–6)? How does God describe the man who trusts in the Lord (vv. 7–8)?

Rewrite the truth from the end of verse 8:

The person spoken of in Jeremiah 17 never fails to bear fruit because his or her trust is in God, and this trust is like a tree planted by water. In part, it's a trust born out of a knowledge of God and His Word, something on which He meditates day and night. Record your findings from Psalm 1:1–3:

What connection do you see between these passages and part of the branch's role in abiding in John 15:7?

Now add in the truths from John 7:37–39. Describe the river of living water you have living in you now:

It was always God's plan for His Spirit to be in you and for the Spirit to be the life source through which you would produce much fruit, even "when the heat comes or in a year of drought" (Jer. 17:9). This fruit happens, dear friend, not because of our own effort, but the life of Christ flowing through us. Now record the fruit that the Spirit flowing through you will produce from Galatians 5:22–23:

> *"Whoever believes in Me as the Scripture says, streams of living water will flow from within him."*
> *John 7:38*

Day 3
The Freedom of Abiding

I can think of only one thing at which I feel I achieved the level of a true champion: striving to change. When I would look at God and His call to holiness, I'd be overwhelmed with everything in me that needed changing. For many years, my time with God and my quest for Him were centered on Him changing me. I wanted to be His fixer-upper project! In fact, that's what I thought our relationship was supposed to be centered on. The problem was, and will always be, that a focus on striving to change kept the focus on me, taking it off of God.

First, I was striving to become someone God said I already was. Record your findings from 2 Corinthians 5:16–21:

You and I are new creations; sin no longer has power over us and a new life—filled with God's Spirit—has now come. God's Spirit is in us. Because of Jesus' atoning death, we have become, according to verse 21, "the righteousness of God." This does not mean there's no longer change needed in my behavior or thought life, but according to Scripture, it's not my job; it's God's job. We simply need to follow and obey Him. Record your findings from the following passages:

Philippians 1:6

Philippians 2:12–13. Note how you work out your salvation:

While obedience to what God shows me is my job, I'm not the project manager. God is. Take a few minutes and ask God what it looks like for you to work out your salvation with fear and trembling. Record the conversation below:

The beauty of God's ordained process is that it is God who works in you to will and act according to His good purpose. I would give God a list, telling Him what we should work on next. (Yes, at least in my head, I really did this!) God's priorities and plans are so different. Recall one of our theme verses, John 17:3: "This is eternal life, that they know You, the only true God, and Jesus Christ whom You sent."

God wants us to know Him and therefore experience the life of living in Him and Him in us. It's through time spent in this relationship—a loving and intimate relationship—that He works in us, pruning us to bring forth the life He has already put in us: His righteousness. It's a beautiful thing. For me, it's been a very freeing truth to know this through first-hand experience. Striving creates and perpetuates self-centeredness and a focus on performance. In other words -- pride. Abiding creates and perpetuates humility. Scripture says humility releases the grace of God: "God opposes the proud, but gives grace to the humble" (James 4:6). Striving creates independence while abiding creates dependence.

To end your lesson today, talk with God about any striving you've been doing in your walk with Him. Or perhaps you're not a striver but have been apathetic toward Him. Simply talk with Him and allow Him to show you anything in your life blocking the flow of His Spirit in you.

> *Striving creates and perpetuates self-centeredness and a focus on performance. In other words -- pride.*

Day 4
The Struggle to Abide

Yesterday we looked at the beautiful relationship and freedom enjoyed with God as we abide and do not strive to produce fruit in our lives. Yet I doubt one of us would deny a struggle can still exist. In our relationship of abiding, God asks us to be still and wait for His timing. Striving is an act of control, even when it's for a godly cause. Waiting is a posture of submission and dependence, which I believe many of us struggle to maintain.

This fact was recently driven home to me as I heard about a couple who waited three hours past their appointment time to be seen by their doctor. I was appalled. While never three hours, I too have had to wait long past an appointment time. Following this conversation and my strong reaction to it, I asked myself, What is it about waiting that is so offensive to me?

I asked this question to two close friends as well. Before I share our answers with you, stop for a few minutes and answer this question for yourself. Why is waiting difficult and possibly even offensive to you? Record your thoughts below:

For my two friends and me, there was an overriding theme of feeling devalued. We felt our time was deemed unimportant and therefore, we were too.

Waiting makes me feel out of control, and I have a tendency to want what I want, when I want it, which usually means now!

Could it be that we are transferring feelings generated by any type of waiting onto God when He, in His sovereignty and love, asks us to wait? Do we feel unimportant and not valuable to God when He asks us to wait? Do we feel He's not in control, possibly because He doesn't care enough about us to be in control? I encourage you to be honest with yourself and God about any struggles you have in waiting. Record your thoughts below:

Now let's take a look at waiting. As we've seen illustrated with Jesus' vine and branch teaching, God's ways with us are often illustrated in nature. A farmer sows a field, and then he waits. A baby is conceived, and then the parents wait. Even a weight lifter will work out for weeks, possibly months, before seeing visible results. Yet in each of these cases, a lot is going on, though it's all unseen.

What could God be doing beneath the surface as you wait?

What crop of fruit could He be birthing?

What trust issue or wall of independence could He be breaking?

Is He giving you an opportunity to praise Him while you wait?

Do you think you could praise Him for the wait?

Let me ask you this: Is He seeking deeper intimacy with you, giving you a longer time to be still (cease striving) and know that He is God (from Psalm 46:10)?

Stillness is a form of waiting. Yet even being still can be difficult for some of us. Certainly our fast-paced society doesn't train us for it. Yet be assured, the evil one would love for the need for quietness and stillness to deter you. He'd love for waiting to defeat you.

We'll end our study today by looking at God's perspective on waiting. As we did in week one, write your thoughts to God after each verse.

> *Do we feel unimportant to God when He, in His sovereignty and love, asks us to wait?*

Isaiah 40:27-31 (NASB)

27. Why do you say, O Jacob, and assert, O Israel, "My way is hidden from the LORD, and the justice due me escapes the notice of my God?"

28. Do you not know? Have you not heard? The Everlasting God, the LORD, the Creator of the ends of the earth does not become weary or tired. His understanding is inscrutable.

29. He gives strength to the weary, and to him who lacks might he increases power.

30–31. Though youths grow weary and tired, and vigorous young men stumble badly, those who wait for the LORD will gain new strength; they will mount up with wings like eagles, they will run and not get tired, they will walk and not become weary.

Day 5
The Joy of Abiding

In late October in Georgia, the landscape changes as leaves, green since spring, turn into vibrant shades of red, yellow, and orange. There's one particular tree on my street whose leaf change I look forward to every year. It's a majestic maple tree whose dark trunk contrasts beautifully with its bright red leaves of fall. It's breathtaking.

Yet I marvel that the leaves, whose change of color delights so many, have done nothing but respond to the changes the tree undergoes in preparation for colder weather. Though these leaves will fall off and bear beautiful green leaves again with the coming of spring, these changes are only the result of the workings in the tree. The branches bear these ever-changing leaves, the fruit of the tree, simply by remaining as part of the tree. I can confidently say that no one has ever heard a tree moaning and groaning to produce its leaves or change their color.

There are times when I will have a thought, reaction, or sense of peace that I know did not come from me. My flesh did not produce this. I know myself well; I've lived in my body more than fifty years, and I am intimately acquainted with my flesh patterns and sinful thoughts. So when the crisis comes and I find myself trusting instead of doubting or when the irritation is directly in front of me and I find myself loving, I pause in amazement. That is not me but Christ living in me.

As Psalm 38:8 describes, I've tasted this life of Christ in me, and I've seen how good it is. This "taste" caused me recently to cry out to God: "I'm so sick of my flesh, of living according to my mind, my will, and my emotions. I'm sick of being so fully consumed with myself. Father, consume me with Your Spirit."

I've tasted and seen that life with His Spirit living and flowing through me far exceeds living this life with my flesh (my mind, will, and emotions) running the show. I believe God when He says in Isaiah 55:8–9 that His ways are not our ways, and neither are His thoughts our thoughts, but they are higher. I am persuaded that surrendering my flesh is far easier than living the rest of my days on earth consumed with and controlled by my flesh. I'm sure I will also need to reread my own words when the resolve I currently hold wavers. The more you and I taste, the more we will want and the stiller we will be.

Jesus told us it would be this way. It was this way for Him, and it is His path of life for us. Read John 12:20–29. Explain below how Jesus describes Himself and what lies ahead of Him, as well as how He modeled a lifestyle of dying to ourselves:

Consider the words of John the Baptist by reading John 3:27–30. Why did he have complete joy?

How does verse 30 explain abiding?

"I chose you and appointed you to go and bear fruit, fruit that will last." John 15:16

Conclusion

"The vine is biologically programmed to channel all its energies and resources into the berries (fruit) so that they may have a better chance of survival." This quote from Wikipedia illustrates how nature parallels God's role in the bearing of fruit. He's made it His job, and He's not enabled the branch—us—to do it without Him.

We do have a role; it's called abiding. God's commands were never designed to be fulfilled in human strength, and the fruit of the Spirit was never meant to be obtained through our striving. Fruit and intimacy were designed to come out of abiding.

Embrace these words of Jesus:

As the Father has loved Me, so have I loved you. Now remain (abide, dwell, live) in My love. (Remembering) you did not choose Me, but I chose you and appointed you to go and bear fruit, fruit that will last. I have told you this so that My joy may be in you and that your joy may be complete. (John 15:9,16,11)

Notes

Week 11
Properly Placed Passions

Day 1
Seeking Him First

As you journey in your intimacy with God, you will find areas of your relationship with God that were once challenging and seemingly out of reach begin to form with ease. This includes spiritual disciplines, such as studying God's Word, praying for others, serving, etc. It's also true in the area of bearing fruit. When we finally stop striving, start abiding, and allow God to do His work in us, fruit will be produced. We will love where we once criticized. We will be patient instead of irritated and impatient. We will have peace where anxiety once reigned. Best of all, we will have joy. We will experience the love, joy, and grace that only Jesus gives as we abide in Him. Recall the words of Jesus: "I have told you these things so that My joy may be in you and that your joy may be complete" (John 15:11).

Though it may not happen immediately, as you persevere in your journey in intimacy with God, a relationship that may even now seem to have little or no taste will one day be like a delicacy from a world-famous chef. God wants you to "taste and see that He is good." Doing so will cause you to see that what you once were content with or settled for was but a stale morsel in comparison. Keep spending time with Him. Rest in the fact that He wants intimacy with you. The taste will come, and it will leave you wanting more, wanting and loving Him above all else!

This week's lesson is titled "Properly Placed Passions." Which one of us hasn't struggled to keep our priorities in line with what God through His Word has laid out they should be? I've certainly struggled to love Him more than I love other people (especially myself) and even other things. I've struggled to seek Him first before I seek or respond to the tyranny of daily life. Which one of us, in trying to develop a new discipline, such as healthy eating, will find much success by spending our time thinking about all the candy we aren't supposed to eat? So it will be with God as we seek Him first, abide in Him, taste His goodness and receive and experience His love. All other passions and pursuits will pale in comparison and become properly placed behind Jesus, our new number-one passion.

Record how these two Scriptures explain this truth:
Matthew 6:33

Galatians 5:16

Process this truth: Think of a current priority or passion in your own life. Often our priorities and passions are good things, but when placed at the top of the list—before God—they usurp the best thing. Begin envisioning how this passion could pale in comparison to an abiding relationship of intimacy with God. Imagine the freedom you would feel. It may help to recall a specific time when you felt especially

> *Often our priorities and passions are good things, but when placed above God, they usurp the best thing.*

close to God. Consider this: What if such intimacy became the norm and everything else fell in place behind it? Write your thoughts:

Our improperly placed passions often block intimacy with God. Sit with God, and ask Him to reveal improperly placed passions in your life. As a child relating to a very loving father, talk to Him about them. Ask Him to "grant you repentance [a change of mind] leading you into a knowledge of the truth" (2 Tim. 2:25). Record the conversation below:

Though not easy, the exercise above is critical for intimacy with God. At our wedding ceremony, I spoke a vow similar to the following:

I, Judy, take you, Nelson, to be my lawfully wedded husband, to have and to hold from this day forward; to love you and cherish you, for better or worse, richer or poorer, in sickness and in health; and forsaking all others, to keep myself only unto you as long as we both shall live.

What past or current circumstance is hindering you from "keeping yourself only unto" God? As you did above, talk with God about it.

Our vow to our bridegroom Jesus should be taken as seriously as a wedding vow, for it is through this commitment that intimacy can grow. Do not be naive about the fact that the evil one will seek to thwart any level of intimacy. Read 2 Timothy 2:25–26, and record your findings below:

As we repent of improperly placed passions, we position ourselves to taste an intimacy never before imagined. It will be a journey far and above any you have ever taken.

Day 2
Love Him First, Part 1

> To know Him
> is to love Him.

> "For God so
> loved the
> world that
> He gave His
> one and only
> Son, that
> whoever
> believes in
> Him shall not
> perish but
> have eternal
> life."
> John 3:16

In 1958, a singing group called the Teddy Bears released a song that would eventually head to the top of the record charts: "To Know Him Is to Love Him." The theme of the song is exactly as the name states, with the chorus saying, "To know, know, know him is to love, love, love him, and I do, yes I do, yes I do." The song echoes a fact stated in Scripture: to know God is to love God. To know, know, know God is to love, love, love God.

Let me show you where it's found. According to Jesus in John 17:28: "I have made You known to them, and will continue to make You known to them in order that the love You have for Me may be in them and that I myself may be in them." Jesus wants us to know God so we will have His love in us. While speaking of His indwelling presence within us, He is also speaking about an internal knowing (grasping, realizing, and experience) of His love for us, as well as in us. Follow this Scripture with 1 John 4:9—"We love because He first loved us"—and we see that to know, know, know Him is to love, love, love Him. The more we know Him, the more we will love Him. It's the purpose of our journey, and it happens in our journey in intimacy with God; a side result is a proper alignment of our passions.

It's a Lifelong Journey

Let's go back to John 17:26. After all He had taught and shown the disciples, there was still so much more about God for them to know: "I have made You known and will continue to make You known." At the time of this prayer to the Father, Jesus was only minutes away from being arrested and carried off to face an unjust trial and crucifixion. Read John 18:1–14. Considering this passage in light of John 17, which we have studied in prior weeks, what do you see about the heart of Jesus?

Jesus came to set the captives free (Luke 4:18), defeat the works of the devil (1 John 3:8b), and give His life as a ransom for many

(Mark 10:45). He came to show us what true love is (1 John 3:16). Ultimately, however, He came because of love—God's love. "For God so loved the world that He gave His one and only Son, that whoever believes in Him shall not perish but have eternal life" (John 3:16).

Especially if John 3:16 is very familiar to you, ask God to speak to you afresh about His love—a love so great that He would give something so great. Record your new insights below:

It's exciting to consider that there will always be more of God to know and therefore always further opportunity to love Him more. Record your findings from Romans 11:33–36:

There will always be more of God's love to receive. Read and then pray Ephesians 3:14-19 over yourself. Record your prayer.

Using the verses below, record a time you have either known God's love in such a personal way, or write a specific prayer asking God to make His love known to you in that way. If you are doing the latter, I encourage you to write the prayer specifically about a current circumstance in your life.

Psalm 86:13, 15

Romans 5:8. Record either a way God demonstrated His love to you while you were still a sinner (before your salvation) or while you were sinning, though you were saved; or ask God to demonstrate His love to you in an area of sin you are currently struggling with.

Romans 8:34–35

I hope you can see from these verses the importance of knowing God's love. Unfortunately, much of the world has not accepted this message: "For God so loved the world that He gave His one and only son, that whoever believes in Him should not perish but have everlasting life." Read John 17:25, and write one reason why:

Lovelessness toward God is often a result of not knowing or inaccurately knowing God. Recalling our definition for the word know, explain why this is the case.

A grave warning is given in Romans 1:21. In this verse, the word know, according to Thayer's Lexicon, means "to become acquainted with." It appears that the level of knowing never went beyond that of an acquaintance. Record below what happened as a result:

In our journey in intimacy with God, our path of life is described in Psalm 16:11. We get to know and then know, know, know Him—and then we taste His love and begin to crave it with an insatiable appetite. End today's lesson by considering any changes you need to make to avoid the deception that comes from improperly knowing God. Next, place yourself in a position to receive God's love as you know, know, know Him. Record your thoughts below:

"Love the Lord your God with all your heart and with all your soul and with all your mind."
Matthew 22:37

Day 3
Love Him First, Part 2

*Hearing that Jesus had silenced the Sadducees, the Pharisees got together.
One of them, an expert in the law, tested Him with this question:
"Teacher, which is the greatest commandment in the Law?" Jesus replied:
"Love the Lord your God with all your heart and with all your soul and
with all your mind. This is the first and greatest commandment. And
the second is like it: Love your neighbor as yourself. All the Law and
the Prophets hang on these two commandments. (Matt. 22:37–39)*

Jesus did not introduce a new command. Read Deuteronomy
6:1–5. These words were spoken by Moses immediately after he had
given the Israelites the Ten Commandments he'd received from God.
It also came after Moses reminded the people that they chose not to
hear God's voice, though God was willing to speak, and asked Moses
instead to speak with God on their behalf.

In love, God seeks to provide for His people. Write out Deuteronomy
6:4 in your own words:

The commandments were God's protection and guide for His
people, enabling them to remain in His love as it was possible in the
old covenant. Record below what Jesus said in John 15:9–12 about His
love, our role in remaining in His love, and the result of remaining
there:

God calls us to love Him with all our hearts, souls, minds, and
strength, not because He needs our love but because loving Him is
best for us. Loving Him protects us from improperly placed passions.
Loving Him brings blessings to us: "Walk in all the ways that the Lord

your God has commanded you, so that you may live and prosper and prolong your days in the land that you will possess" (Deut. 5:33). As in all acts of obedience, obeying the word of the Lord is what's best for us!

Jesus' words in Matthew 22:37–39 were also recorded in Luke 10:27. Consider this command as it is given in response to a different question. Read Luke 10:25-28. What question was asked of Jesus by the expert in the law?

Write the definition of eternal life as we first learned it in week 1:

Though I doubt the Pharisee really wanted to know what it took to not only have eternal life (in years) but the life of God in him, Jesus' answer is nonetheless thorough. From this conversation, what can you glean about how best to not only receive endless years with God but also to experience the fullness of the life of God in you—to experience the fullness of intimacy with Him?

God cares for His children. Loving Him positions us under that protection. It puts us, as David said in Psalm 16:11, on the path of life—the path where there is joy because of God's presence and pleasures untold at His right hand.

Spend some time talking to God about any lack of love for Him and the need for more love for Him.

God calls us to love Him...not because He needs our love, but because loving Him is best for us.

136

Day 4
Delight in the Lord

The line between a passion and a desire is often blurred for me, but there is no denying that I have a lot of desires. I have always desired to have an orderly home. In fact, I can easily overlook a little dirt for cleared-off countertops, picked-up floors, and knowing that all the bills are at least in one place. But while raising three children, organization was not always the order of the day. One day I realized that though my schedule had been quite busy, the order in our home had been maintained with surprising ease. I was pondering this when suddenly a verse came to the forefront of my mind: "Delight yourself in the Lord and He will give you the desires of your heart" (Ps. 37:4). I sensed so strongly God was reminding me of this verse to tell me something. I was seeking Him and delighting in Him (albeit far from perfectly), and He delighted to, in an unknown, supernatural way as only He can, give me this desire of my heart.

For so long I have understood Psalm 37:4 to mean that my desires would become what God desires, and I still believe this meaning is accurate. Yet I am now also fully convinced that as we delight in God and seek to love Him, He will give us our desires when they are in line with His Word and will, possibly for no other reason than we are His children and He delights to do so.

As you seek to love God with all of your heart and delight in Him, I challenge you to look for ways in which He gives you the desires of your heart, as well as ways He changes some of the desires of your heart. If you've had such an experience, please write about it.

"Delight yourself in the Lord and He will give you the desires of your heart."
Psalm 37:4

Work through the following two passages of Scripture and the questions that go with them.

Psalm 37:1–8 has several action phrases (for example, "do not fret" in verse 1). List them below, and then draw a conclusion about how those phrases would apply to your life as a part of your delighting in God.

Now read Jesus' words in Matthew 6:25–34. What should be your attitude toward any unmet desires? What could be the quickest means of either having those desires met or losing the desire all together?

I encourage you to commit Matthew 6:33 to memory. Heeding its instruction is essential in your journey in intimacy with God: "Seek first the kingdom of God and His righteousness and all these things will be given to you as well."

Day 5
Ask For More

There was a time several years ago when I began asking God for more. I wasn't specific about what I wanted more of because I didn't know. I just knew I wanted more of whatever He had to give.

There was a time more recently when I cried out again to God for more. This time I was specific; I wanted to love Him more. After taking an honest look at myself, I realized I had a lot in common with the church in Ephesus in Revelation 2:1–7. I was faithful to God in many ways. I worked tirelessly and persevered without growing weary, but like them, I had lost my first love. In both cases, God answered extravagantly and specifically. In the latter, He worked in me more love for Him.

Loving God above all else often does not come easily, yet God has given us numerous accounts and instructions in the Scriptures of the perseverance He desires from His children. In week 8, we looked at Matthew 7:7–12. Record below how this passage addresses the issue of perseverance. State also God's desire to give us our desires.

Genesis 32:22–32 records an event between the patriarch Jacob and "a man." Read the passage, and then answer the following questions:
Who was the man in this encounter?

What did Jacob demand of him?

What did Jacob get?

It is God's command for us to love Him with all of our hearts, souls, minds, and strength. Yet it is a command that requires His grace for us to fulfill it. Will you wrestle with God to love Him more?

Close your time today with the encouragement of the following two verses. Record your thoughts specific to your life right now below each one.

Philippians 2:13

Philippians 4:19

Conclusion

The television at our house usually airs either the news or a ball game. Whether it shows citizens in a foreign country protesting against their government, college football fans on a fall day, or people with opposing political views, all are filled with great passion.

God created us as passionate people, full of life, who are able to contain great joy and to give and receive much love. Yet His desire is for us first and foremost to be passionate about Him. His desire is also in our best interest and for our highest good. Will you make this your number-one desire?

As I sought God to work in me more love for Him, I would often pray the following verse. I would pray it not because it felt true but both as a request and a statement of faith, believing God would answer my prayer.

As the deer pants for streams of water, so my soul pants for
You, O God. My soul thirsts for You, for the living God.
When can I come and meet with You? (Ps. 42:1–2)

Notes

Week 12
The Joy Exchange

Day 1
Joy Is ... Joy Is Not ...

Welcome to week 12, the final week. Let me begin by saying well done! You've journeyed through much information over these eleven weeks, often studying things that may have seemed to have little relation to the subject of joy. I hope this week you will see the full circle of what joy is, what joy is not, and how we obtain or receive it.

Let's begin by taking a look at how the Scriptures define joy. There are twenty-five Hebrew words (OT) and ten Greek words (NT) used throughout the Bible to represent the English word joy and words synonymous with it. These words are the definitions for each other: joy, gladness, pleasure, and happiness. According to Collins English Dictionary,

Joy is a deep feeling or condition of happiness, contentment, pleasure or satisfaction.[1]

Though a secular definition, I think those are exactly the things God desires us to have. The difference with the world's definition and God's definition is in how we obtain it. Read Ecclesiastes 2, and record below what King Solomon learned from his pursuit of joy, gladness, pleasure, and happiness:

Ecclesiastes 2

On one hand, I read Solomon's words and say, "Well, of course!" On the other hand, I say, "Not so fast." Take a few minutes, and ask God to bring to your mind things you have sought to fill you with joy. Record what He reveals below:

If your list is anything like mine, it didn't include the circumstances of joy described in the following Scriptures. Record your findings from each:
2 Corinthians 8:1–2

James 1:2

1 Thessalonians 1:6 (Note where their joy came from.)

1 Thessalonians 1:6 says that the Holy Spirit gave them joy. Record your findings about this truth from Romans 15:13:

Record the additional insight you glean about joy from the following Scriptures:
Psalm 16:11

Psalm 90:14

From this small sampling of verses and the secular definition of joy on page 1, write your own biblically based definition of joy:

There is certainly no denying the ways in which the world's thinking has permeated my own. I've looked for joy in wrong things and wrong ways and certainly not through trials and suffering. To conclude today's lesson, share with God any misconceptions you've held about having joy in your life. After doing so, write a prayer for any new direction you'd like to take.

Day 2
The Great Exchange

Having largely looked at where joy doesn't come from, today we turn our attention to where it does come from and how we receive it. To that end, I'd like you to ponder the following sentence:

A great exchange occurs by means of the divine exchange and results in a joy exchange.

In week 1, we talked about the divine exchange. We get the life of God in us and unending years with Him in exchange for our lives. As part of this divine exchange, we receive a great exchange—great both in quantity and quality. From Isaiah 61:1–7, record how Jesus found us in the column labeled "Your Life." Then go back through the verses and record what Jesus gave you in the column titled "His Life." Keep in mind that the words can refer to us physically, emotionally, and especially spiritually.

> A great exchange occurs by means of the divine exchange and results in a joy exchange.

Your Life	exchanged for	His Life
V1 poor, especially poor in spirit		A recipient of the gospel message

To experience this exchange, we have to relinquish control of our lives. Considering the list from Isaiah 61, I marvel that I've been so reluctant at times to do so. The life Jesus offers us in this exchange is the life of God in us, as we first saw in John 17:3 during week 1. It's the life Jesus speaks of in John 10:10: "I came that they might have life and have it abundantly."

This exchange is most fully experienced as we believe and see the truth of Galatians 2:20 manifested in our lives. Once again read this verse, adding with it Galatians 5:24–25. Record your insights, this time making them personal:

As Paul ends his letter to the believers in Galatia, he challenges them with strong words in Galatians 6:7–8,14. Read these verses, and then allow God to search your heart and reveal any areas you are withholding from His loving control, causing you to reap things you don't desire.

Be encouraged! Galatians 6:9 says, "Let us not grow weary in doing good, for at the proper time we will reap a harvest if we do not give up." Dear friend, do not grow weary in surrendering all aspects of your life to Christ. Consider the harvest of righteousness you will reap as His life is flowing through you! To conclude today, read Luke 4:14–30. The words of Jesus spoken prophetically through Isaiah in chapter 61 were spoken personally by Jesus on one Sabbath in the

> Galatians 6:9 says, "Let us not grow weary in doing good, for at the proper time we will reap a harvest if we do not give up."

synagogue in Nazareth. As you read this account, try picturing the scene in your mind.

Tradition holds that the rabbi in charge of the synagogue would ask one of the men to read from a scroll. As news about Jesus, their hometown boy, had spread throughout the whole region, I imagine their interest was piqued, and they must have hoped to see what all the hype was about. Not coincidentally, the rabbi handed Jesus the scroll of the prophet Isaiah, and He selected the text in Isaiah 61. No doubt He read the passage with great authority. Jesus then handed the scroll back to the attendant and sat down. At this time, the one to read could also begin to teach. Having captured their full attention, Jesus said some astounding words to all of them: "Today this Scripture is fulfilled in your hearing."

Jesus offered them a great exchange. It was a great exchange brought about through the divine exchange, which would have resulted in a joy exchange. The Jews gathered in the temple that day knew well the words Jesus read. They knew who He was claiming to be, but they simply didn't believe Him. This is an issue we will look at tomorrow. In the meantime, consider again that a great exchange occurs by means of the divine exchange and results in a joy exchange. Let's not miss it!

Instead of their shame My people will receive a double portion, and instead of disgrace they will rejoice in their inheritance; and so they will inherit a double portion of their land; and everlasting joy will be theirs. (Isa. 61:7)

Day 3
Free to Believe

We ended yesterday with Isaiah 61:7—the promise of everlasting joy as we exchange our poverty of spirit, brokenness, mourning, and shame for the fruit of the life of Christ in us, freedom, gladness, comfort, and praise … Yet we cannot deny that joy eludes many Christians, and when it does come, it is often fleeting. We will look at the reason for this today.

Our journey into joy through the life of Christ in us is much like the nation of Israel's journey to possess the Promised Land. In God's

> *Like the Israelites, who saw literal giants, we often see the circumstances in our lives and think joy isn't possible for us.*

eyes, the land was theirs: "The LORD said to Moses, send some men to explore the land of Canaan, which I am giving to the Israelites" (Num. 13:1). God also says the freedom to live a life of joy is ours: "It is for freedom that Christ has set us free" (Gal. 5:1). Jesus did not lie in John 15:11 when He said that the joy He has can be in us, making our joy complete.

Like the Israelites, who saw literal giants (Num. 13:27–33), we often see the circumstances of our lives and think joy isn't possible for us. In doing so, we become like the people who gathered in the synagogue while Jesus publicly proclaimed Himself to be the long-awaited Messiah; we simply don't believe Him. In doing so, we never enter into the land of joy God has made possible for us, just as was true of the nation of Israel.

Consider again these verses from John 15:9–11.

As the Father has loved Me, so have I loved you. Now remain in My love. If you obey My commandments, you will remain in My love, just as I have remained in His love. I have told you this so that My joy may be in you and that your joy may be complete.

The key to joy is to remain in God's love. The key to remaining in His love is to obey Him. The key to obeying Him is to believe Him.

Recall our study of John 6:25–29 in week 3. In response to the question, "What must we do to do the works God requires?" Jesus said, "The work of God is this: to believe in the one He has sent." I am deeply challenged by Jesus' words, and I wonder if a radical change would take place among all who call Jesus Lord if we focused our attention on simply believing Him. After all, we do call ourselves believers. I feel confident in saying that belief is essential for the joy of Christ to be in us and for our joy to be complete.

This truth is expressed in the following passages also. Record your findings:

Romans 15:13

1 Peter 1:8

Just as joy may elude us, so often will belief. Yet there is great hope, for God has made a way. Just five verses before our last Scripture reference in 1 Peter 1:3, the key begins to unfold: "Praise be to the God and Father of our Lord Jesus Christ! In His great mercy He has given us new birth into a living hope, through the resurrection of Jesus Christ from the dead."

I'm going to lead you on a trail of verses to show you how God often overcomes unbelief.

Write out 2 Corinthians 5:17:

If you are "in Christ," you now have access to the wisdom of the Holy Spirit. Read 1 Corinthians 2:6–16, and record your insights below:

You have been given the mind of Christ, meaning you have the ability to discern truth. Truth discerned and applied becomes belief. Record how this truth is expressed in John 8:31–32:

Most often God uses His Word to give us His mind, for His Word expresses His mind. Read Hebrews 4:12–13, and record all that is available to you through God's Word.

> *I feel confident in saying that belief is essential for the joy of Christ to be in us and for our joy to be complete.*

You have a living hope! If you will offer yourself to Him, God will transform your thinking (Rom. 12:1–2) and take you from unbelief to belief. This is freedom—freedom to experience the everlasting joy that is yours. Paul also wrote in Galatians 5:1, "It is for freedom that Christ has set you free." He goes on to challenge them to "Stand firm, then, and do not let yourselves be burdened again by a yoke of slavery." That is my plea to you. As a new creation, unbelief and all that seek to block you from living a life of joy have been exchanged for the mind of Christ. A great exchange occurs by means of the divine exchange and results in a joy exchange.

As we close today, take joy in these words of Isaiah 61:7 once again:

Instead of their shame My people will receive a double portion, and instead of disgrace they will rejoice in their inheritance; and so they will inherit a double portion of their land, and everlasting joy will be theirs.

Psalm 42

Day 4
Living a Life of Joy

God desires His children live lives of joy! This is easier to grasp once we understand that joy has nothing to do with our circumstances and therefore isn't contingent on a lack of suffering and trials. In seeking to live lives of joy, the psalmists can teach us a lot. Read Psalm 42. Sorrow is certainly not lacking in this psalm. Record below some of the phrases in which the psalmist expresses his sorrow:

What is the possible cause of his sorrow?

According to verse 5, what is the psalmist's expectation in the midst of his sorrow?

What does the psalmist do to overcome his sorrow?

How does this relate to what we studied yesterday about belief?

What can you learn from the psalmist about living a life of joy, even in the midst of sorrow?

Letting Joy Overcome a Different Kind of Grief

Nehemiah was the writer of the often-used phrase: "The joy of the Lord is your strength." He was a man who certainly experienced this truth. His heart grieved over the ruin that had befallen Jerusalem and the shame it might bring to the name of God. He cried out to God on behalf of the city and its people. God heard and answered, using Nehemiah, with the help of an ungodly king, to rebuild the wall around Jerusalem.

"When the seventh month came and the Israelites had settled into their towns, all the people assembled as one man in the square before the Water Gate. They told Ezra, the scribe, to bring out the Book of the Law of Moses, which the Lord had commanded for Israel" (Neh. 8:1). The people stood for hours listening to Ezra read. They worshiped God with their hands lifted up and their faces bowed to the ground. The Levites explained to the people the meaning of all that was read, making it clear so they could obey. Then Nehemiah, the governor of Judah, stood in front of the assembly of people. He addressed a people weeping as they listened to the words of the law, saying, "This day is sacred to our Lord. Do not grieve, for the joy of the Lord is your strength" (Neh. 8:9).

With Jerusalem's walls rebuilt, why do you think the people were grieving?

It's likely their grieving was over their past disobedience to the law and for their sins. At times our remorse comes not because of circumstances beyond our control but those that occurred because we kept control, not relinquishing it to God. We, like the Israelites, can choose to let joy be our strength in this. If you find yourself grieving a past sin, take this time to let the joy of the Lord be your strength. Record a prayer to God below:

In 2 Corinthians 12:9–10, Paul wrote about an area of suffering in his life and concluded that in his weakness, Christ's power came upon

> *We, like the Israelites, can choose to let joy be our strength.*

him. Consider this passage along with Nehemiah's encouragement to the people. What encouragement can you draw regarding a lack of joy you may be experiencing?

Just like Paul, the people felt weak, and though they felt weakened in their sorrow, their weakness was still an opportunity to receive God's strength. For us, as it was for them, strength can come as we choose joy. That's where we'll pick up tomorrow.

Day 5
Joy: It's Possible

We concluded yesterday with the words, "For us, as it was for them, strength can come as we choose joy." So how do you and I choose joy? We do it just like David did: we choose to remain in God's presence.

You have made known to me the path of life. You fill me with joy in Your presence, with eternal pleasures at Your right hand. (Ps. 16:11)

The path in the "path of life" David speaks of is the Hebrew word *orach*, and it means a literal road or a course; it was the road of travel of his life. (See also week 1.) We are all on a path of life, but the choice is ours. We can experience joy and pleasure on that path by choosing to live in the presence of God.

In week 1 you were asked to write your thoughts to God after each verse in Psalm 16. I ask you to do that again today. I encourage you to work through this exercise slowly, giving God time to speak and bring to your mind new truths you have learned. At the end, you may want to go back and compare your answers, though I encourage you not to do so beforehand.

My prayer is that you will see a marked difference in what you wrote this time as compared to when we first began the study. I pray

> We are all on a path of life, but the choice is ours whether we experience joy and pleasure on that path.

that you have traveled further down the path in your journey of intimacy with God.

Psalm 16 (AMP)

1. Keep and protect me, O God, for in You I have found refuge, and in You do I put my trust and hide myself.

2. I say to the Lord, You are my Lord; I have no good beside or beyond You.

3. As for the godly (the saints) who are in the land, they are the excellent, the noble, and the glorious, in whom is all my delight.

4. Their sorrows shall be multiplied who choose another god; their drink offerings of blood I will not offer or take their names upon my lips.

5. The Lord is my chosen and assigned portion, my cup; You hold and maintain my lot.

6. The boundary lines have fallen for me in pleasant places; yes, I have a good heritage.

7. I will bless the Lord, Who has given me counsel; yes, my heart instructs me in the night seasons.

8. I have set the Lord continually before me; because He is at my right hand, I shall not be moved.

9. Therefore my heart is glad and my glory [my inner self] rejoices; my body too shall rest and confidently dwell in safety,

10. For You will not abandon me to Sheol (the place of the dead), neither will You suffer Your holy one [Holy One] to see corruption.

11. You will show me the path of life; in Your presence is fullness of joy, at Your right hand there are pleasures forevermore.

Conclusion

In week 1, I shared with you how this study was named. It came through the revelation that the only way to experience true joy is to have an intimate relationship with God. At the time, I wasn't seeking joy but the absence of pain. I've come to realize that no matter what I'm seeking, my priority must be walking in intimacy with God. Otherwise I am selling myself short of the abundant life God created me to live. Putting anything ahead of this pursuit causes me to sacrifice a tremendous amount of joy. Can you say this with new conviction?

This is eternal life (in fact it's the only thing that makes up true life) that I know (intimately, through first-hand, experiential knowledge) the one true God, and Jesus Christ whom He sent (John 17:3).

If you can, then you are on your way to discovering, as King David did, that our joy and pleasure in this life come from being in the presence of God.

You have made known to me the path of life; You fill me with joy in Your presence, with eternal pleasures at Your right hand (Ps.16:11).

May God grant you a daily realization and manifestation of this truth in your life.

God bless you!

Notes

Will You Linger a Little Longer?

Whether he's asking about my day or how one of our kids is doing, there is one word my husband prefers not to be given as an answer: fine. It tells him nothing, he says. As I approached mid-life and found myself describing life as fine, I better understood his angst with the word. One day I asked a friend who was a few years older than me, "Is this what mid-life is like? The lows don't seem as low, but the highs don't seem as high." She too thought it might be so. Yet deep in my heart, there was a gnawing thought—surely there's more! Granted, there have been numerous times when fine would have been a relief, but an ongoing fine somehow didn't seem right.

While I was pondering this one day, the second half of John 10:10 came to my mind: "I came that you might have life and have it to the full." My heart leapt! Of course there's more. Jesus came for us to have an abundant life, a full life, a life that is overflowing. I had to learn this lesson one more time. There is joy in His presence and eternal pleasures at His right hand (from Ps. 16:11). Though some of the things that used to excite me in my youth may no longer hold the same appeal, there are unspeakable joys and pleasures I have yet to experience. They are all found in God's presence as I journey in intimacy with Him. They all reach far beyond fine.

Consider the words of Ephesians 3:19: "And to know this love that surpasses knowledge - that you may be filled to the measure of all the fullness of God." As we walk more deeply into intimacy with God, we know—through first-hand experience—His love, and it is a knowing far beyond only head knowledge. As a result of knowing His love, we are "filled to the measure of all the fullness of God." How can life be merely fine with the fullness of God alive in us? It's the only ingredient you and I need for an abundant life.

You've been given a kingdom-engraved invitation to intimacy with God. I hope you've been challenged and inspired to pursue it. I pray that the two weeks we spent looking at God's invitation to intimacy has shown you that no matter what lie or hindrance has kept you from it, God wants intimacy with you! I also hope you've discovered that any investment made for intimacy with God yields a return far greater than anything this life has to offer. Understanding the barriers has been pivotal in my journey. Even though I'll constantly need to nurture my trust and dependence on God, I am overwhelmingly thankful for the ground gained because of the numerous ways God has given me first-hand experience with Him as trustworthy and dependable.

While our journeys in intimacy will look different, there are God-ordained practices to spur us on. The twenty-minute praise challenge is something I go back to regularly. When discouragement or grumbling seek to set in and distance me from God, twenty minutes of praise is an amazing remedy. In addition, listening as well as speaking (no more coffeehouse scenes for me) in my times alone with God has been a blessing beyond measure and has provided a means for deeper intimacy beyond anything else.

Finally, I marvel at the benefits and blessings God pours out on His children through a relationship of intimacy. By the grace of God, I'm not the striver I used to be. There is still room for improvement, but when I consider what He's done so far, it gives me great confidence in God's promise in Philippians 1:6: "Being confident of this, that He who began a good work in me will carry it on to completion until the day of Christ Jesus." The apostle Paul found great joy in this promise, and I do too! Then when I stop and ponder the great exchange God offers me on a daily basis—my brokenness for His wholeness to name just one—I am overjoyed to the point that my heart struggles to contain it. Whatever God offers, I want it!

I know you could write your own summary as well. In fact, that's exactly what I encourage you to do. Go back through the weekly lessons, and give God the opportunity to show you all He has done in you.

Then, as one last exercise, turn it all back to God in a chorus of praise.

God bless you!

Judy

Glossary of Key Terms

The following terms are used throughout the study. Understanding their full meaning will help you grasp the truths found in the Scriptures that possess them.

Eternal Life

The life of God in you and endless years in duration with Him. The very life of God, of which believers are made partakers.

Faith/Trust/Belief

Reliance on the integrity, strength, and surety of a person or thing; to have confident expectation and hope. Throughout the New Testament, the words faith, trust, and belief most often come from the same Greek word pistis. The words are inseparably linked and combined give a fuller definition.

Intimacy

An affectionate, loving and personal relationship with another person. The feeling of belonging together; having a detailed knowledge and deep understanding of one another. The absence of walls or fences.

Know

Knowledge gleaned through first-hand (personal) experience, connecting theory to application through direct relationship. Knowledge obtained through ongoing exposure and experience. To make known. Also used for sexual intercourse.

Repentance

A change of mind. A turning away from unbelief, mistrust, and rebellion against God. Turning toward complete reliance upon His forgiveness and favor on account of Christ.

Path of Life

Has a two-fold meaning: a way of living as well as the literal journey we travel and experience in living. It refers to God's way of righteousness and the paths we can choose, leading to life or leading to death.

Endnotes

Week 1

1. Retrieved (in part) from p://dictionary.reference.com/browse/intimacy?s=t. June 2, 2012.

2. Hebrew Greek Key Word Study Bible. (Grand Rapids, MI: AMG International, Inc., 1996), 1602.

3. Ibid., 1580.

4. Ibid., 1630.

5. Ibid., 1651.

6. Ibid., 1520.

7. Ibid., 1505.

8. Retrieved from http://www.biblegateway.com/passage/?search=Acts%2017:17-34& version=NIV. August 2011.

Week 2

1. Hebrew Greek Key Word Study Bible. (Grand Rapids, MI: AMG International, Inc., 1996), 1544.

2. Retrieved from http://ancienthistory.about.com/library/bl/uc_bakaoukas4d2.htm. August 2011.

3. Ibid.

Week 3

1. Retrieved (in part) from http://dictionary.reference.com/browse/trust?s=t. June 2, 2012

2. Hebrew Greek Key Word Study Bible. (Grand Rapids: AMG International, Inc., 1996), 1662.

3. Ibid., 1520

Week 4

1. Hebrew Greek Key Word Study Bible. (Grand Rapids: AMG International, Inc., 1996), 1644.
2. Retrieved (in part) from http://dictionary.reference.com/browse/independent?s=t. June 2, 2012.

Week 5

1. Retrieved (in part) from http://oxforddictionaries.com/definition/praise.   June2, 2012.
2. Retrieved from http://library.timelesstruths.org/music/Turn_Your_Eyes_upon_Jesus/. June 1, 2012

Week 6

1. Hebrew Greek Key Word Study Bible. (Grand Rapids, MI: AMG International, Inc., 1996), 1602.

Week 8

1. Hebrew Greek Key Word Study Bible. (Grand Rapids, MI: AMG International, Inc., 1996), 1619.
2. Ibid., 1686
3. Ibid., 1639

Week 9

1. Hebrew Greek Key Word Study Bible. (Grand Rapids, MI: AMG International, Inc., 1996), 1651.

Week 12

1. Retrieved (in part) from http://www.thefreedictionary.com/joy. June 2, 2012, and http://dictionary.reference.com/browse/joy?s=t. June 2, 2012